DON'T TURN BACK

Don't Turn Back

A Reassuring Road Map to Navigating Divorce after Abuse —Legally, Financially, and Spiritually

LYDIA DOMINGUEZ

Contents

True Vine Publishing
Don't Turn Back/Lydia Dominguez- First Edition, 2021

Cover Design by Christopher R. Vasquez

ISBN/SKU 978-0-578-90899-1(Paperback)
EISBN 978-0-578-90900-4 (E-Book)

This book is intended to provide general information and resources for domestic violence victims. The information provided in this book is not intended to substitute for legal
advice delivered by an attorney. Readers are encouraged to
speak with an attorney before taking legal action. The information on this book is NOT a substitute for legal advice. Talk
with a licensed attorney to get legal advice on your situation.

The conclusion and opinions expressed in this book are those
of the author. They do not necessarily reflect the official po-
sition of the United States Government, Department of Defense, or the United States Air Force.

Dedicated to the women who seek the light in the midst of darkness.

Foreword

If you are currently enduring a toxic or abusive relationship, you are not alone. Millions of women find themselves in these dire circumstances and wonder how to free themselves—and what will happen to them when they do. This book is for battered women who are prepared to put in the work to escape an abusive relationship and prosper. If this is your situation, or that of someone you know, this book is for you. This is your survival guide for regaining your sense of dignity and self-worth. It will also provide you with the tools you need to move on and never turn back. Allow me to act as a trusted friend, taking you aside in private, and offering you sound, practical advice.

Each woman's path is different. At one end of the spectrum are women who fear for their lives because their partner is physically violent, psychologically abusive, or both. At the other extreme are women who are simply beginning to question their long-term personal happiness with the partner they've chosen. There are lots of situations in between. Only you know your situation and the many nuances it entails.

Everyone's timing is different as well. Some women are just beginning to question their current situation, while others have been working hard for a long time—on their own or with their partner and/or a counselor—to find a way forward separately.

Wherever you happen to be on your journey, I hope the information, lessons, stories, and strategies I share here will be of value to you. Many of the things I write about come from my own experience, some from the experience of others I've talked to, and some from experts. All of it is shared in the hope—the *belief*—that you will come out the other side of this experience stronger, smarter, and happier than you were before.

Just as there are no perfect marriages, there are no perfect divorces. Let go of what you perceive to be the "right way" to leave your relationship, the "right time" to do so, and the "right amount of time" to spend on healing from this relationship. Explore your options, and find the best solutions for you and your family. You will have to make tough decisions along the way, especially if you have children to factor into the equation. If you're lucky, both you and your partner will want what is best for them. If that is not the case and you must fight on behalf of your children to keep them safe, you will need a strategy for you and your children's life transition. That's when it is time to call in the experts for help.

I wrote this book for women who are ready to escape an abusive relationship. Although I developed this book for women, men may be in abusive relationships as well. I do not intend to exclude men from reading this book; men are just not the focus.

My goal in writing this book was not to be the only expert you need. Divorce is a complex process; therefore, you are likely to involve lawyers, counselors, financial advisors, and other professionals to assist on your team. To begin, and to know what steps to take, you must prepare yourself emotionally and intellectually for the process. When you are subjected to trauma and suffering, you must repair your wounds in ways modern society cannot. You must understand your feelings and those of your children, and you must have a grasp of how the process works.

This is where *Don't Turn Back* comes in as a useful tool. Well before I researched and considered writing this book, I went through my own divorce. My own story—although it is singular and undoubtedly different from yours—underpins everything in these pages. My personal experiences are the reason I wrote this book in the first place. I wrote this book as if I were having a painfully straightforward and loving conversation with a friend, with no hint of judgement or persecution.

I spent years suffering in silence and felt alone in my situation. I clung to a relationship that was becoming more and more violent and unhealthy every day. *Why don't I just leave?* I remember asking myself. When I look back on it, I know it was because I didn't see a way out. When you can't see a path, you can't follow one. If I can illuminate your path out of a constricting and harmful relationship, then I have done what I set out to do. Something worthwhile and valuable will have come from my own bad situation. Every suggestion I make in this book is based on practical sense and useful information.

I hope the ideas and information I've gathered here help you turn the page on an abusive relationship and propel your life in a new direction. But first, you must turn the pages in front of you and read with an open mind and a heart full of love for yourself. Why? Because even though I don't know anything about your specific situation, I do know one thing:

You are worthy of love.

—Lydia Dominguez, September 2020

Chapter 1

Love

"Love is patient, love is kind. It does not envy, it does not boast, it is not proud. It does not dishonor others, it is not self-seeking, it is not easily angered, it keeps no record of wrongs."

—THE APOSTLE PAUL, 1 CORINTHIANS 13:4–5 NIV

Why sugarcoat it? Divorce is a dark, ugly, lonely place. Whatever gut punches—literal or figurative—you may have survived during your marriage, you must now survive a different kind: blows to your self-confidence, self-esteem, and self-worth. When domestic violence is part of your divorce story, as it was for me, you may find yourself in another level of pain you didn't expect.

Leaving a relationship is hard, and you should feel proud of yourself for accomplishing it, but deciding to leave is just the first step. Divorce proceedings may take twice the amount of time you'd hoped and double or even *triple* the amount of money. And you can't begin to know the emotional toll it will take on you and your children until you experience it. As hard as this transition is, though, I'm here to tell you the good news: There is a light at the end of the tunnel. I've seen it. It's real.

There is a different you waiting on the other side of your divorce. She will be battle-scarred, for sure, but those scars are part of her story. *Your* story.

What could *I* possibly know about *your* situation? Good question. I keep talking about you as if I know you, but the person I know best is myself. So . . . before I make any more assumptions about *you*, I want to share a little of my own story. My goal is not to overshare, make you feel uncomfortable, or elicit your sympathy. My goal is to bring home the three overarching messages of this book:

- You are not alone.

- You are worthy of love.

- You will survive.

For most of my ten-year marriage, I worked hard at holding onto the good times while overlooking the bad as much as I could. It seemed like for every ten bad things my ex did, he'd do one good thing (offer one gesture of love and warmth) and that is what I would cling to. When I looked at him, I concentrated on seeing the man I knew he could be rather than the man he was. I saw a man who was vulnerable. I saw a man with potential. I saw a man who needed a good and steady woman to lift him up.

In order to protect his ego and encourage that better man to emerge, I molded myself into a smaller version of me. I supported him in everything he did and showed him what unconditional love looked like. Eventually, the real me—the bigger me—got lost in his shadow until I couldn't find or even recognize my true self. My dreams, wishes, and desires slowly slipped away as our marriage was completely filled up by *him.*

Even as I realized this, I told myself I didn't mind. I was in love. I'd made a commitment, and I was happy to see it through. Deep down, I knew the balance between us was off, but I figured it would get better if I could help him get better.

But things didn't get better. On the contrary . . . they got much, much worse. Our marriage has deteriorated gave my repeated attempts. It was as if my ex stopped trying to be on his best behavior. Over time, I watched him slowly take off his mask and someone dark and unfamiliar appeared. If he didn't like the way I was doing the chores, then instead of gritting his teeth or slamming a door, he'd verbally abuse me by calling me names. On one occasion, he poured disinfected cleaner on my head from behind. If I had the nerve to try and stand up for myself (often I didn't even try, but occasionally I did), he'd resort to physical violence. At first, he wouldn't actually hit me; instead, he'd punch a wall next to my head or throw something in my general direction.

It may not surprise you to know that eventually those blows landed on me. He didn't hit me every day, or even every week at first, but it became a regular occurrence soon enough. Over and over. Each time he hit me, a little voice inside my head told me it was my fault, not his.

He'd never do something like that on purpose. Maybe if I hadn't talked back. Maybe if I'd kept the house a little neater, the kids a little quieter, done and said things just right, then he wouldn't have lost his temper.

Sometimes he apologized later; other times he didn't. Either way, I honestly believed each "episode" was my fault. He kept me off balance, confused. His moods were unpredictable, and so were his actions. All I knew was that I loved him, and I loved my kids. This was my life, and I had to figure out a way to make it work.

I know now that what I felt for this man may once have been love, but when he began abusing me, and that was long before he became physically violent, what I felt was no longer love. I felt many other things (fear, confusion, desperation, longing, obligation) but not love.

I don't want you to think I was completely passive or helpless. I attempted to leave him *seven times* throughout our twelve-year relationship. Each time, I was determined never to go back—until I did. But I didn't know then what I know now. I didn't know how many women faced the same horrible decisions I did, or what they could do about it. I didn't know about the resources out there to help someone like me. I felt alone, ashamed, and powerless to do anything but turn around and go back. Each time I returned to my toxic and dangerous marriage, I repeated to myself, *I know who he really is. This isn't him.* I truly believed I saw the man he could be. My goal was to figure out how to bring that good man out instead of seeing the good in myself first.

Of course, I know now that he could never be that man, at least not with me. My salvation would not be in changing him but in breaking free of him.

Here's the truth: My marriage didn't end with me bravely walking out the door. It ended when my husband stole our money, discarded me, and filed for divorce. The irony is, when those things finally happened, it was after a period when we'd been relatively happy. He'd seemingly transformed into the warm, loving husband and father I'd always wanted him to be, at least on the surface. He was different—until he wasn't. Until his mask came off again.

In the end, he admitted he was living a lie and dumped me. I felt like garbage on the side of the road—ugly, unwanted, and unworthy of him or anyone else. I believed him until I got healthier and stronger and *woke up.* Today, I can say he did me a favor by leaving me, but at the time it caused me to question every single thing about myself.

You've heard it a thousand times: a good marriage is based on love. But what is love? I realize it can mean different things for different couples, but a few things are certain. Love does not hurt. Love does not mock. Love does not hit. I know this and you know this.

Women in abusive relationships may not realize they are being abused and manipulated right away. In my case, it took me some time to admit it to myself. And when we *do* realize it, we may need some time to figure out how to act on what we know.

In case you are wondering about the "who, what, and where" of abuse, here are some facts to begin to enlighten and support you:

- Despite how it may be portrayed in the media, abuse pervades all classes, races, and cultures, regardless of financial status or education.

- Most victims—at least 76 percent, according to the National Coalition Against Domestic Violence (NCADV)1—are women.

- Some ten million people in America are victims of physical violence each year.

- Abuse is a pattern, not a one-time occurrence.

- Assaulting someone is a crime. Domestic assault constitutes a felony or misdemeanor in most states, regardless of the fact that the perpetrator may be a spouse, boyfriend, relative, friend, or acquaintance. Whether it happens rarely or on a daily basis, physical violence is a crime, and it is never acceptable.

In any circumstance, leaving is the most dangerous and hardest part of a woman's transition. False starts, like the seven I experienced, are common. There are a lot of reasons why a woman might return to an abusive relationship: fear of being alone, of losing custody of the children, of being broke, of being judged by others. Often, there is that underlying, desperate belief that the abuser really can change. Many believe that the abuser's love is true even though his actions are unspeakable.

I resisted seeing myself as a victim, survivor, or battered woman. *That's not me*, I thought. Yes, I had bruises, but what constitutes a *beating*? What does it mean to be *battered*? Finally, there came a point where I had to face facts. I had to draw the line. I couldn't survive if I kept holding on to my abuser, any more than a person being dragged behind a car can survive by clinging to the side mirror.

As I began to research answers to my confusion, pain, and Post Traumatic Stress Disorder (PTSD), I discovered I wasn't suffering alone. I read story after story of other women's pain and realized I didn't deserve it either, and I certainly didn't deserve to be abandoned. No one does!

When I began the process of separation and divorce, I never dreamed it would take over two difficult years to complete. I learned so many lessons in that time, and much of what I learned is recorded here for your benefit. None of these lessons was a solution in itself, but the more I learned, the more I healed. Eventually, I learned enough to enable me to move past the abuse and pain and blossom into my own person. I recovered my strength and self-esteem. I was no longer the weak woman my ex had made me believe I was. Once I could separate who I was from who he wanted me to *believe* I was, I could take back control of my life.

All of this is important, but the first and most important thing on your journey out of your toxic relationship is your physical safety. If you are reading this and are in immediate danger of abuse, you must take action through the assistance of professionals to stop it. There will be time for healing, but you must survive first!

If you are in immediate danger, call 911.

If you are in need of support—but neither you nor your children are in current danger of physical harm—the National Domestic Violence Hotline[2] is available by calling **1-800-799-SAFE (7233).** The hotline provides lifesaving tools and immediate support to empower victims and survivors to find safety and live free of abuse. Highly trained expert advocates are available 24/7 to talk confidentially with anyone in the United States who is experiencing domestic violence, seeking resources or information, or questioning unhealthy aspects of their relationship.

Chapter 2

Safety

"A woman is like a tea bag: You never know how strong she is until she gets in hot water."
—ELEANOR ROOSEVELT

No matter what phase of divorce or separation you are in, you need to formulate a plan for your physical and emotional safety. Remember: the most dangerous time for a battered woman is when she leaves. This is the time when you are taking back power and control over yourself, and your abuser knows this. According to a National Violent Death Reporting System (NVDRS) report published July 2017,[3] over half of all female homicide victims are killed by a close or intimate partner. When you read the statistics, it suddenly becomes a bit easier to take the first step into your new life. Though uncertainty will reign, deep down you know there is no other choice you can make but to plan your exit. It will take courage. What is courage? Courage is doing the right thing even though you're not sure how things are going to work out.

Your first priority in this phase must be to get yourself and your children to a safe place. That takes some planning, and so does your life after that. When you make a safety plan tailored for you and your children, it's important to be practical and understand your limitations. If you've thought things through, you can fall back on your step-by-step plan when fear and tension take over and when it's hard to think straight.

Before you leave your partner, carefully consider who you can trust with your life and the lives of your children. Who can you talk to without fear that the conversation will get back to your partner? Start reaching out to trusted friends and family. Talk honestly with them, even if you don't feel like sharing all of the gory details. Ask them for whatever help you think they can provide. Anyone close to you may already have suspicions that something is wrong. They may already want to help but don't know how—or even how to raise the subject. Give them an opening, and you will be surprised how generous they might be.

Is there someone you can stay with for a while until you get back on your feet? Even if it's hard to ask, do it. The worst that can happen is that they will say no, in which case you can then ask someone else.

Of course, you also have to think about how you will finance your transition. If all of your money is held jointly by you and your partner, he might try to cut you off from it. While you can, you must gather money of your own that he can't touch. This takes prior planning.

- Open a new bank account in your name only, and put in as much money as you can afford without raising suspicion. This can be all at once or over time.

- If a new bank account isn't practical, hide cash somewhere that only you have access to, or give it to a trusted friend or family member for safekeeping.

- Buy Visa or American Express gift cards if that seems like the best way to have your own source of cash. To disguise the purchase on your account, get a pre-paid card or obtain cash-back at large retail stores.

- Money can also be hidden in the pantyliner pocket of women's underwear.

- If you're employed, find out if your employer has a credit union from which you might take a loan. This way, you can gradually it pay back from your paycheck.

Finally, if your financial situation is dire without your partner's support, look into services such as shelters,

Medicaid, food stamps, housing authority, and welfare. See if you qualify for food banks, free school lunch programs, and community charities. These programs were designed to aid people like you, and there is no shame in seeking these benefits when you are in need. While a shelter may seem like a drastic step, keep in mind that they are best suited to provide you with services you might need at the moment. Determine what resources might be available to you during this difficult time. You'll see how these services will help you escape an abusive relationship with peace of mind.

Angel Flight West arranges flights for victims of domestic violence to relocate to a safe location. Please bear in mind they mostly fly within the thirteen western states but will consider requests outside of their region on an individual basis. Check out www.angelflight-west.org, for eligibility requirements to participation in their flight program.

It's absolutely crucial to think clearly and use your street smarts to insure you survive until you can reconfigure your life.

Once you know where you are going to land and how you are going to finance your life temporarily, there are other things to think about.

- Keep track of your phone and computer (or whatever technology you have) at all times. Always keep your devices fully charged! If your partner frequently looks at or takes your phone or computer, keep a record of the important information. Back up personal data in platforms such as Dropbox that have password protection. Also, be careful what you say in texts or emails. Remove GPS apps, and disable locations for you and your kids on Find my iPhone.

· Take a picture of your partner's vehicle and license plate. You may need it later.

· Keep your gas tank full and your car parked facing the street so you can get away quickly, if necessary. If you suspect your ex is tracking you, self-inspect or take your vehicle to be inspected for a tracking device.

· Make sure your children know their address, phone number, and your full name. You can help them learn these facts by turning them into a song.

· Teach your kids what to do when your partner gets violent. Instruct them to move far away from the room where the violence is occurring and then to call 911 to report the situation. You'd be surprised how resourceful even very young children can be when they have to.

Because I brought up the subject of kids, I want to take a minute to talk about their well-being, as it's something that concerns all moms contemplating leaving their partners. We've talked about your fear, but what about the fear your children are experiencing? If you are afraid, then they certainly are too. They need your reassurance that everything will be alright. Find a time when you are alone with them and explain the situation in a way they can comprehend. Obviously, that will depend on their ages and ability to understand. Don't overload them with relationship details. What they really want to know is:

· Why are things changing?

· Where will we live?

· Will we still go to our same school, have our same friends, and keep our toys, belongings, and clothes?

· Will we be safe?

· Will we ever see Daddy again?

Even if you don't have all the answers, be as reassuring as you can be—without lying. Take it from me, your children can tell when you aren't being honest. The most important thing of all is that they feel loved and safe, even if you are fighting your own fears and concerns.

It goes without saying that you want what's best for your kids, and that might include finding outside help for them in the form of professional counseling. Make it part of your plan to look into state-funded resources for your kids' mental state—and your own too!

Pets can be like our children, and they often get caught in the middle of family breakups. Do you have pets? Do you plan to take them with you? If so, you'll have to include them in your exit strategy. Whether you are taking them or leaving them behind, try to get any necessary vaccinations or checkups out of the way, and make sure each pet is registered in your name. Save copies of their medical records in your phone, car, or work computer. Some states allow battered women to keep their pets in shelters with them until they can find housing—but we'll get to the subject of shelters later. Contact your local women's shelter[4] to ask for information about whether they accept pets or not.

Are you pregnant? A pregnancy makes the situation a bit more complicated. It may also add to the tension of an already stressful household. Prenatal appointments are a good place to talk about your situation honestly and ask for help. Gather your strength and level with your obstetrician. Doctors are an important link in the chain that connects abuse victims with professionals whose job it is to protect them—including law enforcement. When you make a claim of abuse to your doctor, it is recorded in your medical record and the police are notified. Don't be afraid of this process; it was designed to protect you and your children, born and unborn. It, like any other system, is flawed; nevertheless, you should make use of all accessible resources.

While we are on the subject of law enforcement, I hope you know that you should call the police whenever an act of abuse occurs. You may be planning to leave, but until you do, it's important to report all acts of violence and get them on the record. Police involvement can de-escalate the situation and may save your life. And later, if you find yourself in family court, the judge will rely heavily on evidence such as police reports, medical reports, letters from counselors, and school employees.

Once you have gotten your plans in place (meaning you know where you are going to go and how you are going to take care of yourself and your kids for a while), it's time to make your move. The reality is, you may have to leave with very little money, very few belongings, and a lot of questions about the future. But you will be leaving with your life, and that is Priority One.

- Plan to leave at a time when your spouse is not home.

- Take all of your identification cards, your birth certificate and your children's birth certificates, everyone's passports, Social Security cards, medical records, car title, and deed or rental agreement for your home.

- Pack as many clothes and personal items as you can comfortably transport and keep with you, including some of your kids' favorite things and items that have sentimental value for you—jewelry, or even a photo album. But don't go crazy. This isn't the last time you'll have access to your belongings.

Once you've made the leap and are physically separated from your partner, the hard part is over, right? Well . . . not quite. Now you have to stay safe—and that begins with setting boundaries. The majority of states have a Confidentiality Address Program (CAP)[5] designed for victims of stalking, domestic violence, and sexual assault. Each state runs the program differently, but overall, they allow victims the use of a fictitious mailing address to maintain confidential records. They offer certain protections for survivors of abuse, including a legal "substitute" address (P.O. Box, usually) victims can use in place of their physical address. This includes when an address is required by public agencies, such as a driver's license, and voter registrations. Check your local laws, which vary state by state.

This reduces the risk of being tracked through public records. Some states also allow participants in the CAP program to register and vote by absentee ballot without revealing any physical address. The program is funded differently in each state, so it may not be publicized very well. See the references at the end of this book for more information.

Does your partner know where you are? If so, you'll want to limit your interactions with him until you feel stronger. If you have to see him (in court, during child exchanges, at your office, at the kids' school), keep the interactions brief and simple. Do not let him bait you into old fights. Try to keep things cool and calm and get away as quickly as you can. Often, an abusive spouse wants to feed the flames of conflict just to stay engaged with you. But it takes two to fight. In the book *Becoming the Narcissist's Nightmare*, author Shahida Arabi details how to interact with and disarm an abusive, narcissist partner. She describes how victims of these toxic relationships forge trauma bonds with their partners that involve actual chemical changes within their brains similar to those experienced by habitual drug users. These bonds make it particularly difficult for the victims to leave because they feel chemically connected to their abusers. Shahida goes on to describe how to disarm a narcissist, get away from him, and then overcome your deep-rooted feelings of shame and worthlessness. This is a book I wish I'd read sooner, and I highly recommend it to you.

Even though you are out of the house, it doesn't mean your partner won't try to come after you or your children. There are systems in place to help prevent this—or at least prevent it from happening repeatedly.

If your partner is interfering with you or threatening you or your kids, particularly physically, and if you fear for your safety, you are entitled to a protective order. That is a court-issued document, delivered to your abuser officially, that can be used to stop or prevent threats, harassment, or physical injury. This may seem harsh (and there is no guarantee he will abide by the order), but it is an important thing to do. It will become a critical part of your story when you move forward with separation, divorce, and custody issues. If your abuser does defy the protective order, you are within your rights to call the police and have him prosecuted accordingly. In fact, you must, if you want satisfaction in family court later on.

Your children have a right to be safe from your partner as well. Your lawyer (we'll talk about the legal process in the next chapter) can advise you of your kids' rights and protections.

Before we leave the topic of safety, I want to share a few more tips for protecting yourself throughout the process of leaving your relationship:

- Once you've relocated, you might want to clue in your neighbors. Show them a picture of your ex's vehicle and license plate, and inform them that he is not welcome at your residence.

- Make sure your new locks are secure and that you know where all the keys are located.

- Consider putting up security cameras to keep track of who comes and goes. These can be very comforting, especially while you are getting used to being on your own. It is now legal for footage from these cameras to be used as evidence in court of violations of restraining orders.

· If you have tangible concerns about altercations with your ex, you can ask the police to patrol your area when he is due for a visit, or on nights when altercations may have occurred in case your abuser circles back around for more taunting.

As carefully as you plan things, and as certain as you are that you are doing the right thing, you will experience a gamut of emotions after you leave your house. Fear and anxiety may move in and become your roommates. You will probably wonder if you've done the right thing—for yourself and for your kids. You might find yourself thinking about going back, trying again, and toughing it out. Sometimes it might feel easier to retreat from the unknown and go back to the familiar. *It wasn't really that bad*, you might say to yourself. Those bad memories seem to fade at this point. *Maybe it will be better now. Maybe he learned from his mistakes.*

Those feelings and fears, those doubts and second thoughts are natural, but they aren't useful. That is why I developed this book: to assist you in overcoming your anxieties and launching your new life. If I can do it, I'm confident you can too.

The Criminal Justice Research Center at The Ohio State University investigated what is commonly known by prosecutors and victim advocates; witness tampering is a serious issue in domestic violence cases.[6] Live telephone conversations between domestic violence offenders and victims were utilized in this research to address unique concerns regarding how and why victims decide to recant and/or decline prosecution. They performed a qualitative research with 25 heterosexual couples in which the male offender was detained (in the United States) for felony-level domestic abuse and made phone calls to his female victim during the pre-prosecution phase. This study examined: 1) interpersonal processes related with the victim's desire to recant; and 2) the pair's formulation of the recantation plan after the victim planned to recant. Their findings revealed that, across couples, the perpetrator's pleas to the victim's compassion through accounts of his mental and physical difficulties, awful jail circumstances, and life without her had the greatest impact on the victim's desire to recant. The perpetrator's purpose was strengthened by the couple's invocation of thoughts of life without each other, as well as the perpetrator's minimizing of the abuse. When the victim decided to recant, the pair devised a recantation strategy that included reframing the abuse incident to protect the perpetrator, blaming the state for the couple's split, and exchanging detailed directions on what should be said or done.

Why do I mention this study? Women return to their abusers so often that lawmakers have changed some laws so they can continue to prosecute abusers even without express cooperation from their victims. They shouldn't have to do that! This is, nevertheless, reality.

Even though your emotions are all over the place, there is only one right answer. If your abuser is in jail or being prosecuted for domestic violence you need to have the courage to stay away from him, guilt free, without regret or shame. You are not responsible for his actions.

In my own case, I wasted too much precious time trying to remain in a toxic relationship with someone who couldn't love me or treat me well. Don't make that mistake! Out of wishful thinking, I recanted the abuse and ended restraining orders. This pushed me back in terms of both time and money, as well as in the courtroom. Once you take that first step out, you will be that much closer to gaining the dignity, self-respect, and passion for a new life you deserve.

Chapter 3

Legal Help

"A sense of urgency comes from a powerful connection to the present."

—ROBERT GREENE, THE 33 STRATEGIES OF WAR

Not all divorces are created equal, and they are bound to become more complicated when they include issues of domestic violence and/or substance abuse. While there are certain cases where lawyers are only a tangential requirement, such as in amicable, uncontested divorces between two people with no children and very little property, most divorces require legal representation on both sides. Divorce should not be a DIY affair any more than surgery. You wouldn't take out your own tonsils, right? Dissolving a marriage requires the professional assistance of a good attorney.

I can imagine what you are wondering: *How much is this going to cost? Where am I going to get the money?* Among all of the misgivings you might have about leaving your marriage, one of them might be the cost of dissolving it—and that cost is real. But not all attorneys wear fancy suits and charge top dollar. And not all of them demand a hefty retainer fee up front. Do some research. When you talk to various attorneys, ask them frankly about their fees. If money is really an issue, investigate local legal aid options within your state. WomensLaw.org[7] is an excellent site I've discovered. Despite the name, they provide information that is relevant to people of all genders, not just women. Their *email Hotline* will provide legal information to anyone who reaches out with legal questions or concerns regarding domestic violence, sexual violence, or any other topic covered on their website. Keep in mind that every county offers some free legal aid,[8] though funding has been sparse in recent years. I suggest looking into what's available in your area by checking out: www.lsc.gov/what-legal-aid/find-legal-aid to search for assistance in your county. These attorneys might work for a low cost or no cost at all. Or talk to an attorney about building his or her legal fees into the settlement you get from your ex. In any case, I beg you not to hesitate in moving forward because of legal costs. This is an investment in your own bright future, and it is a necessary one.

The laws governing divorce vary from state to state, and they are not simple. Your attorney will help you understand what you are entitled to and will work with you to make a plan for getting the best deal you can, financially and in terms of child custody. Additionally, local lawyers are acquainted with the judges they appear before. They know their quirks and preferences and can tailor their strategy to help acquire the judge's favor (or at least understand) your side.

You will probably be asked to speak before the court on your own behalf. If this happens, your attorney will coach you in what to say and what not to say. You'll even be coached on what to wear. Your children might be asked to speak, and they'll need to be coached by your attorney too. But the most important thing about having good counsel is knowing that someone smart and experienced has your back in what might be the toughest courtroom battle you'll ever face. I can't emphasize this enough: *Find a good advocate who will be your warrior, your sniper, and your voice.* There are times in life when we can't succeed on our own, and this is one of them.

Finding a divorce attorney can be tricky. Ask close friends who have recently been in similar situations to share their experiences and who they used. It's fine to research lawyers online, but it can be tough to narrow down the choices this way. So, think hard about what you need and expect from an attorney, and don't be shy about it. Once you have a few names, call them and ask for a consult, which should be free. Talk to at least three attorneys, and trust your instincts about who you feel can represent you effectively.

What should you look for in a potential attorney?

· When you walk into his/her office, look around. Is the office busy, tidy, well-organized? Do clients seem to be waiting endlessly, or is the business run efficiently?

· Look at the attorney him/herself. Is he/she sophisticated, polished, well-spoken, and confident?

· In your conversation, does the attorney answer your questions effectively, honestly, and directly? Does he/she listen and respond to you personally or spout rote answers? Is he/she patient and probing or abrupt and dismissive? You definitely want someone who treats you as an individual (not a "case") and exhibits respect and compassion as well as a thorough knowledge of the law. That being said, remember: your attorney is neither your therapist, your counselor, nor your best friend. Your attorney is your advocate and voice. A businesslike demeanor is a good thing, not a bad one.

Let's get back to the uncomfortable subject of money. As I said earlier, you may be concerned that you can't afford an attorney. Really, though, you can't afford not to have one. So, ask the tough questions and get the full picture about fees. If the attorney you want requires a retainer, a lump sum up front to start your case, you might need to find a way to get it. Once again, you may need to approach family or friends for a loan, or go to your credit union or bank. At the same time, don't be shy about asking the attorney to work with you on a payment plan or contingency fee (paying him or her from the money you collect from your ex). There are very few times in life when it is a good idea to go into debt or spend money you don't have; hiring a divorce attorney might be one of the times you go against typical schools of thought.

I want to guide you a little further in working effectively with your attorney. It's hard to know what questions to ask if you don't understand the laws governing divorce in your state, so lean on your lawyer to help you see your situation clearly. Here are some specific questions you can ask:

- What is "community property" in my case, and what already belongs to me? What does the law say about how our belongings and money will be divided up?

- With your knowledge of the local courts, how long do you think the divorce process will take?

- What, exactly, are the laws governing child custody, child support, and alimony? In my case, what do you see as the best arrangement and best outcome for these three categories?

· How often will we communicate about my case (phone calls, emails, monthly in-person meetings, texts)?

· Can you provide me with an estimate of how much my case will cost based on what you currently know about my situation?

· What can I do to help control the cost of the divorce?

· Can I seek to recover any legal fees from my spouse?

· Are you ready for a strategy session?

Of course, you will think of many more questions of your own as you prepare to move forward. As they occur to you, write them down and take them to meetings with your attorney. That will keep you focused and ensure that your sessions are efficient and reassuring. I also urge you to read up on local divorce law.

Be aware that your lawyer will have a lot of questions for you as well. In order to build your case, he or she will need a clear and detailed picture of your marriage, your finances, and the entire history and foundation of your marriage. These questions may sometimes feel invasive, and the work of assembling all that information can be daunting, but the more facts and figures you can put together, the better job your lawyer can do in advocating on your behalf. If you are well organized, your case will go smoothly and cost you less money and time. Here's an example of the kinds of questions attorneys may ask you during the initial consultation:

- What assets do you own in your name?

- What is your income? What is your current estimated value of your assets and debts?

- List relevant dates, such as marriage date, separation date, and children's birthdays.

- Provide any information you have regarding the other party's income, financial situation, employment, and mental health record.

- What is your work schedule, and how does that impact your need for childcare?

- Who primarily cares for the children daily?

Before we conclude the issue of legal aid, I strongly advise victims of abuse to obtain legal support; nevertheless, you also have the option of fighting this legal struggle on your own. I've witnessed women struggle to explain their message or submit the incorrect forms over and again. All of this might lead to delays or convey conflicting messages to the family court judge. That being said, every family court has a self-help center. This center is available exclusively to self-represented parties. The self-help center in your county can provide education, information, legal forms, community referrals, and other support services to self-represented parties in family law proceedings. The staff is unable to offer legal advice. They cannot tell you whether or not to file a case, what to file, recommend a specific attorney or law firm, offer an opinion about your case or predict how a judge will decide, speak to a judge on your behalf, or tell you what keywords to use in your court documents or at a court hearing. The staff at the self-help facility is required to maintain neutrality. Be forewarned; there is no attorney-client privilege or confidentiality for any information given by a guest at the center.

Chapter 4

Financial Independence

"Divorce is one of the most financially traumatic things you can go through. Money spent on getting mad or getting even is money wasted."

—RICHARD WAGNER, COMPOSER

In order to begin stabilizing your life into a new normal, you will need to get control of your finances from the beginning. Life after marriage can feel like survival of the fittest, and your finances are a major aspect of your "health and fitness."

Whether you are still in transition or have landed in a place of your own, it's important to start paving your financial foundation. If you didn't do so before you left, go to your local bank, preferably one you have done business with before, and open a new checking and savings account in your name only. Don't feel obligated to ask for permission, or even to let your ex know about it. Just do it! As an adult, you do not need consent from anyone to manage your own money. It's probably safest to choose the option of paperless statements, since you may not yet have a permanent address at which to receive mail. (You certainly don't want your ex intercepting your statements.)

If you are employed and your paychecks are set up to be deposited directly into a bank account, make sure they are not going into an account you share with your ex. The minute you have a new account number, change your direct-deposit instructions with your employer. Or, if it works better for you, change your payment method to paper checks until your new account is active. The goal is to move totally away from any involvement in joint banking.

It might seem as if I am dwelling a *lot* on your finances. I understand you are hurting inside and are likely thinking more about your sense of personal loss than the financial challenges you face. But trust me when I tell you that the two are very much entwined. That void you are feeling isn't just the loss of your relationship; it's a hole in your wallet as well. Finances play a huge role in your ability to gain stability in your new life.

To think clearly about your money situation, you must assess exactly how much you have saved and how much is coming in each month. Include your wages, benefits, and any payments you may be receiving from your ex. Then you must take a hard look at your expenses. These include rent, utilities, insurance, credit card payments, loan payments, and school or daycare fees. Don't forget the money it takes to care for your family: food, clothing, entertainment, school supplies, kids' doctor visits, gas for your car—everything. You have probably already itemized all of this for your lawyer, but make sure the list is accurate.

Is your monthly income enough to cover your monthly expenses? If not, can you supplement it with money from your savings without running through it too quickly? It's always best to keep some savings, but if this is that "rainy day" you've been saving for, so be it! You can start saving again when you are back on your feet. If your bills are overwhelming, your ex should be helping—but this can take time to sort out and enforce legally, and you have to live *now*.

If you are new to managing your household money, you aren't alone. Lots of women exit a marriage with very little knowledge about how the money stuff works. During the first year of my divorce, I finally learned how to file my taxes. Be assured . . . you can learn. I hope the word *budget* doesn't scare you because budgeting is the first step.

All a budget really consists of is a list of expenses in order of importance—starting with things like rent, food, and utilities, then working down to optional things, like movie tickets and ice cream for the kids. Acclaimed author and radio talk-show host Dave Ramsey frequently refers to your key budget items as your "four walls." When in a crisis, he advises us to go back to basics. Budget first for food, second for utilities, third for shelter, and fourth for transportation. If you have to file for food stamps or housing assistance, so be it. As I said earlier, there is no shame in taking advantage of these beneficial programs. The key point is that you must overcome your fear of handling money and get past the instinct to seek permission from others. Deep down, you know what is best for your newly configured family (or yourself, if you are on your own). Trust in your survival instinct to make it happen.

You might need some help. There are experts who specialize in helping you restructure your expenses and debts and pay them off slowly without your creditors coming after you. There is nothing more stressful than ducking calls from creditors demanding to be paid, and you do *not* need that stress during this time. Every state has a fund called the survivor benefit, typically funded with money forfeited by convicted felons. These payments compensate you for any medical bills or property damage arising from documented abuse. Go to your local Victim Witness Program at the local police department for more information regarding your state's specific guidelines.

For more resources on survivor compensation in cases of domestic violence, visit www.compass.freefrom.org. This tool is designed to help you pursue options in each state to cover some costs of the harm you have experienced.

Now that you are on your own, you'll need to work on having a good credit score as an individual. The first thing to do is request your credit report and see where you stand. If all of your finances have been joint, you may not have much of a credit profile. And if your ex has been lax about paying the bills, your score may be adversely affected. How can you begin to repair it? Make sure you have both a checking and a savings account, and that both have money in them and are never overdrawn. First and foremost, learn to be intentional with your money. It might take some time, but eventually you can create (or rehabilitate) your financial profile and send your credit score up to a level where you can qualify for a car loan, a home mortgage, or other money that can help stabilize your life. Be patient with yourself on the money front though. Rome wasn't built in a day, and the deeper the hole you are in, the longer it will take to climb out.

While you are examining your credit score, make sure your ex isn't taking advantage of you by taking out loans in your name, charging up credit cards you are responsible for covering, or moving money that should be in your joint account into his own account. Even those who once loved us can start to feel "entitled" to rob us in these situations, and that includes identity theft. Becoming financially literate is a way to empower yourself. It takes confidence anddetermination, but you can do it. Do not allow yourself to be trapped by a barrier of money; this will only serve to keep you in a cycle of abuse.

Here's another really important thing to do. No matter how much chaos is swirling around you right now, take a half hour or so and *change all of your passwords.* If you're like me, you have a lot of them. The more time you spend online, the more passwords you have, and each and every one of them should be changed at this point. Create passwords that won't be easy to guess, like your kids' or pets' names. Each account should have a different password—no sense in using the same one for every account because it only sets you up for hacking. Since you probably can't remember separate passwords for each bank account, email account, social media account, or credit card account, write them all down in a very safe place. It shouldn't be on your desktop or in a file labeled "passwords." (Sounds silly, but people do that!) Better yet, use one of the many apps designed to securely store passwords. You must understand how important it is to keep your identity secure, and that starts with vigilance about the online business you transact. *Change your passwords, and don't reveal them to anyone.*

In a 2012 nationwide survey conducted by Mary Kay, Inc. called "Truth About Abuse,"[9] the residents of 733 domestic violence shelters were polled. A whopping 74 percent of the women admitted that they'd stayed with their abusers longer than they should have for financial reasons. Money is not a good reason to put yourself or your children in danger. Now that you've broken free, it's time to reclaim control of your finances, whether you're living in a shelter, an inexpensive housing complex, a friend's house, or your own home.

I recommend listening to the National Domestic Violence Hotline's video series called *Women Breaking Free: Stories of Strength from Survivors of Domestic Violence*, featuring Suze Orman. Orman is a well-known financial advisor, television and podcast host, and author of ten consecutive *New York Times* bestsellers about personal finance. Orman uses the stories of real women to teach lessons about financial freedom, and the knowledge she imparts is not only empowering, it is also inspiring. You can find the video on the National Domestic Violence Hotline YouTube page titled, "Women Breaking Free."

Chapter 5

Business Matters

"We make our own plans, but the Lord gives the right answer."

—KING SOLOMON, PROVERBS 16:1 NLT

There's more to reframing the business of your life than opening new bank accounts. For one thing, update your will! Too many people forget about this important step—though a good lawyer will remind you to do it.

Make whatever changes you want to it so that it is appropriate for your current situation and reflects your wishes. Then have a new one drawn up, signed (by you), and witnessed. It will automatically take the place of any prior documents, so you don't have to worry about destroying any previous wills.

If you have minor children and don't believe your ex would be a fit guardian if something were to happen to you, you should make arrangements for who will care for them if you die before they reach the age of majority. I know this is a difficult thing to think about, but it's part of being a responsible parent. There are legalities here. Your ex has certain rights, and you need to understand them. However, if you have any reservations about your ex becoming sole parent in the event of your incapacity, you should see a specialist and find out what you can do about it. Particularly if your ex was abusive to your children. If there is someone you'd want to take up your job as guardian, such as a parent or sibling, you'll need to talk to them about it and make sure they're on board. This is a touchy subject, I know. But it is something that all single, separated, and divorced parents must consider. And before we leave the subject, this applies to your pets as well. Legally, pets are considered "property," not dependents, but you should think about who you'd like to inherit them and get their commitment. Include this information along with your will and healthcare proxies. (We'll get to those in a minute.)

In addition to a revised will, you need to make sure your beneficiary designations are up to date. If you have a life insurance policy, IRA, or certain other kinds of bank accounts, you have probably designated beneficiaries for those monies, and chances are, you named your spouse. If you don't want your ex to get that money, you have to change those designations. Don't put this off!

While you're at it, you'll want to assign someone you trust to be the executor of your estate. *Estate? But I don't really have much*, you think. Doesn't matter. Whatever you have at the time of your death, including both assets and debts, are part of your estate, and somebody will need to sort it all out.

I grew up in a Mexican-American family in El Paso, Texas, and in my culture, life insurance was considered very bad luck. My parents and grandparents believed that getting life insurance could bring down a curse or *brujos*—a very serious matter. I don't mean to make light of cultural traditions, but I have come to believe that life insurance is far from bad luck. In fact, it is a good thing to have—for the sake of your own well-being and the future of your family. As it says in Proverbs 13:22 (esv), "A good man leaves an inheritance to his children's children."

We're all going to die someday—not soon, we hope—and I can't tell you how much happier I feel knowing that my kids will be taken care of financially in the event of my premature death. With apologies to my family, I know that getting my affairs in order will not make me die sooner. Nor will having a will, a living will, and a healthcare proxy—so let's talk a little about those.

- A **last will and testament** is a legal document that tells others how you want your property and other assets to be handled after your death and includes family responsibilities, such as who will assume legal guardianship of your children.

- A **living will** is a legal document that outlines your personal preferences for end-of-life medical treatment.

- A **medical power of attorney** (medical POA or health POA) is a legal document that authorizes a person of your choosing to make tough medical decisions for you in the event you are incapacitated.

If your estate is small and simple, and you prefer a more do-it-yourself process, you can probably create or update your will and these other documents by using resources you can find online. Personally, I believe it is worthwhile to consult an attorney (at least for recommendations). Updating your beneficiaries involves simple phone calls or visits to your insurance company and banking institutions—no extra help needed there.

Here are a few resources for free or low-cost legal aid to ensure your legacy and wishes are carried out so that you are protecting your family and gaining peace of mind.

- Dave Ramsey's "Start My Will," in collaboration with Mama Bear Legal Forms: mamabearlegalforms.com.

- Do Your Own Will: This is 100 percent free: doyourownwill.com.

· Total Legal: for $19.95, you can create a will, or you can sign up for a membership plan for as little as $7.49 per month: totallegal.com.

During my research for this book, a friend told me a terrifying story about her own family. Unfortunately, her stepmother died quite suddenly, and it turned out that she hadn't updated the beneficiary designation on her insurance policy since her first marriage. Even though she had been divorced from her ex for fifteen years, he collected her entire death benefit, which was a whopping $50,000! Although he must have known it wasn't what she wanted, he refused to share any portion of the money with my friend, her sister, or their father. Already devastated emotionally, the family faced a new form of trauma in that they could barely afford to bury their mom and move forward.

I hope this illustrates how important it is to get your personal business in order as part of the process of beginning your new life. Any time there is a major change in your situation, it is worthwhile to look at these documents and make sure they still reflect what is in your heart. Nobody is privy to the contents of your will except your attorney—who has the original locked away and is sworn to confidentiality—unless you choose to share the information with others. You will want to review it, and probably change it, immediately after every life-changing event, such as a birth, a death, a marriage, or a divorce.

Chapter 6

Getting Help

"Divorce is a marathon not a sprint."

—ANONYMOUS

There was a time, in the midst of my divorce, when I called my mom every day to complain about my life. I'd complain about the dishes piling up, about trying to find time to go grocery shopping, about struggling to help the kids with their homework. One day, Mom had heard enough. "Stop complaining," she told me in that no-nonsense voice of hers. "Suck it up, buttercup. You're not the first woman to do this, and you won't be the last. You can do it!"

Her words were like a slap in the face! Here I was, seeking sympathy and some kind of acknowledgment of my pain and suffering; instead, I got a stern wake-up call. But you know what? It didn't take me long to realize it was exactly what I needed. I am not a victim, and neither are you. We are survivors. My mother was right. I needed to get over my own victim mentality and press on. I needed to stop worrying about all that I might be doing wrong and start focusing on the fact that I had to be the hero of my own life and a superhero to my kids.

I also had to let go of the perfect image of single motherhood I had in my head based on what I'd seen on TV and in the movies, or just in my own imagination. I might never be the perfectly put-together, organized, wise, and level-headed woman I wanted to be—an unflagging example of strength, courage, and success for my kids. But I can still be a good mother who creates a loving, safe, and happy home for my family. So, what if the laundry basket overflows sometimes or the best meal, I can put on the table comes in a bucket? So, what if I sometimes close my bedroom door at night and cry into my pillow at the loneliness I feel?

In the early days of our new life, when my kids looked at me with real fear in their eyes about all that still felt uncertain and new, I learned to ask myself, *are we better off now than before we left? Are we safer and happier? Do we have a better chance for a successful life?* And the answer was always a resounding *YES*. I had to learn to let that be enough.

I also had to learn new ways to ask for help and lean on the people who genuinely cared about me or had important guidance to offer. When you have a husband or partner, it's easy to rely on him for everything. When he's no longer in the picture, you can't survive on your own. You have to find support—from family, friends, and professionals.

Maybe your ex always took care of the car or the plumbing. What happens when you need an oil change or your toilet overflows? You find someone who can help, that's what! And that someone should *not* be your ex. That's a habit you need to break before it gets started. Needing someone to fix your car doesn't mean *you* are failing—just the car!

As much as we fret about the encroachment of technology in our lives, it can save us time and energy in numerous ways. Technology isn't just social media and games; it's a tool to assist you in your daily life—so use it. No time to shop and your kids are eating out all the time. Look into grocery apps that facilitate online ordering and delivery of everything you need. Some companies charge fees for delivery, but you can save by paying for a monthly, unlimited free-delivery pass that will pay for itself if you order at least once a week. You can even set up standing orders for things you need all the time and schedule a weekly delivery slot that suits your schedule.

While we're on the topic of online ordering, think beyond groceries. There's almost nothing you currently shop for that can't be ordered online and delivered, including pet products, toilet paper—you name it. If there's a chore you'd like to streamline or delegate, and the cost fits within your current budget, look for help online.

I mentioned the car earlier, but I want to go back to that because car care seems to be a particularly stressful topic among newly single women. (You may be one of those women who loves to look under the hood and get grease under her nails, but if so, you are in the minority!) Unless you live in a city where driving isn't a necessity, your vehicle is probably your lifeline. It connects you to friends and family, gets you to work, ferries your kids to school and activities, and helps you cart all of your essential stuff from here to there. You need a safe, reliable car almost as much as you need a roof over your head. Which means you need to take care of it.

In the midst of my own chaotic, newly single life, my faithful Camry suddenly started making loud, metal-grinding noises. Before I could figure out what to do about it, it lost its ability to accelerate. *What the heck, car? Why would you betray me?* Of course, the car wasn't betraying me; it was the other way around. Overwhelmed with my job, court dates, and full-time parenting, I'd forgotten to check the oil! I was way overdue for an oil change, and the damage was done.

Maybe you can imagine the looks I got from the men in my office when I told them what had happened. This lapse cost me $2500 for a new (used) car—the Camry was shot! I never forgot about the oil again, partially because I put a reminder in my phone calendar. Yep, technology to the rescue again.

In those early days, so many things around my house fell apart that it was comical. Or it seems comical now. At the time, I felt like a failure. The ceiling fan in my son's room crashed to the floor (luckily, while he was in the living room), my back fence fell apart, my garbage disposal died . . . It seemed as if every day brought a new disaster. What did I do? I drank a glass of wine, of course. But then I got myself together and found a good handyman. In your post-marriage life, you might be surprised to find that your handyman becomes your "hero"—at least for a while. So, ask around, look online at sites like Home Advisor or Angie's List, or go "old school" like I did and check out the bulletin board at the local hardware store. Whoever you hire, though, make sure he is insured and bonded, and *get an estimate for the work up front.* And, hey, if money is tight, you can always get creative and think about ways you might be able to exchange for services. If you know a guy who is great at fixing cars, but his kid needs help with schoolwork, exchange some tutoring for some repairing. We hear every day that we are in a "barter economy" now, so take advantage of it.

On days when it feels like your world is falling apart around you, remember this: You are more capable than you realize. You are not alone, and he is not the only person with a set of skills and a pair of capable hands.

Chapter 7

Law and Order

"One word of truth shall outweigh the whole world."

—ALEXANDR SOLZHENITSYN, NOBEL PRIZE IN LITERATURE 1970

Separating from an abusive partner is three times tougher than any other type of divorce, physically, emotionally, and lawfully. As you continue on your journey toward healing, I feel it's important to emphasize that, in order to rebuild your life, you must have zero to minimal contact with your abusive spouse. This will help you get through the difficult court hearings that might involve details of your domestic violence issues and use of alcohol or drugs. Dwelling on matters of violence and substance abuse can take a serious toll on your strength, and you don't need that.

You may already know that there are two kinds of divorce: uncontested and contested. But just in case you are still in the early stages of the process, here are some quick definitions. An *uncontested divorce* can be filed when all parties agree upon matters involving separation of assets, child custody, and spousal support. Uncontested divorces usually go through fairly quickly with the help of skilled divorce attorneys and/or mediation sessions. While there are benefits to an uncontested divorce, sometimes it is impossible to come to an agreement about important matters with your soon-to-be ex-spouse, and that means you are headed toward a *contested divorce*. This is where each party retains separate counsel to either negotiate a settlement or enter into a lawsuit. Either way, you will find yourself going to family court, probably more than once.

Family court judges see hundreds of divorce cases every year and expect everything to be properly prepared and neatly presented. Your lawyer will be the first one to tell you that judges don't want to hear bickering or sob stories; they want to hear coherent arguments backed up by legal principles. They want to see well-constructed legal documents with evidence and facts that leave little room for questions. Now do you see why you can't do this on your own?

The majority of family court hearings last less than five minutes, but a trial can last hours or even days. Needless to say, the expense of it all mounts up quickly. This is why, even if you and your spouse disagree, it is better to attempt to reach an agreement, some type of compromise that you can both live with. Attorneys and mediators want that for you as well, and the good ones will guide you toward settling. That said, you have to stand up for what is rightfully yours, even if it means an unpleasant court battle. Each case is different, so my best advice for you is to find a lawyer you trust and work closely with him or her until you have what you need and deserve from your soon-to-be ex.

Family court judges don't want to see your journals or listen to long stories about what happened between you and your husband. These things are considered "hearsay." In other words, something you *say* happened but have no proof or evidence to back it up is basically your word against your husband's, and that's just a waste of time in court. Another thing to understand is that it doesn't much matter who is to blame in cases of divorce. What really matters in a trial is the *verifiable* truth, what you can *prove*. Keep to first-hand accounts by describing what you saw and experienced. Don't bring up rumors or secondhand information since they can't be proven in court. Never diagnose or refer to your ex in disparaging words in any court documents or in front of a judge. Your lawyer will help you stick to the facts, in both documents and testimony.

Things like medical reports, police reports, and doc-ument photographs of your injuries if you have been abused are useful as evidence, which is why I advised you earlier to get these things and keep them safe. Your testimony in court will serve to bring the evidence to life. But if you don't have it, your stories won't have a firm foundation to rest on. Other things that can serve as evidence are letters from schoolteachers, reports from counselors, and bank statements.

Speaking of bank accounts, a big part of your case will hinge on money and assets. Whatever money and property you and your husband have amassed during your marriage has to be divided between you both. Who gets what? Laws governing what you are entitled to vary from state to state, so your lawyer will have to fill you in on the particulars. Your goal will be to get what you deserve and not one bit less.

Of course, your spouse's attorney will try to protect and advocate for him as well. For the most part, it's best to let your attorney and his attorney hammer things out rather than mixing it up with your soon-to-be ex when you see him in the courthouse hallway or during meetings where you are both present. In a range of emotions, your ex can be manipulative about what assets he feels you are entitled to. Don't take his word for it. Do *not* discuss your case with your ex. If your case is going to trial—or even if you're still trying to negotiate a settlement—your lawyer will probably tell you to keep your interaction with your spouse to a minimum. Besides not wanting the stress of those conversations, you don't want to "tip your hand" and let him know your strategy. There will be an accounting done of all marital assets, as well as all sources of income. Does your husband make the majority of the money? If so, he might be responsible for paying you alimony as well as child support. If you make more than he does, it could go the other way. Child support payments, if any are mandated, are affected by these things as well as by your custody arrangement—another factor that has to be sorted out.

Yes, it can be a lot to think about. It isn't my goal here to explain all the ins and outs of divorce law to you. My goal is to help you understand what the issues are and what questions you might want to ask your attorney as you look at your situation and goals. He or she will ask you to think about a lot of these things in depth, but you might as well start the process now and envision what you consider to be the best outcome for you and your children. In the end, you may not get everything you want, but you definitely won't get it if you don't know what *it* is!

In addition to all the other lists you are going to have to make, be sure to keep an itemized list of your court costs and all of the expenses associated with your divorce. Stay organized, store all your receipts in a binder, or electronically on a Google drive. (If your divorce goes to trial, the costs really mount up.) Your biggest expense will be your attorney's fees, but there may be other things too: investigator fees, expert witness fees, even lost wages from having to make court appearances. Once the divorce is finalized, one party may be responsible for the other's court costs, thus those expenses may come into play later.

Are you wondering about those investigator fees I mentioned? Yes, I'm talking about hiring a "private eye." It's more common than you think, and your lawyer can tell you if it is advised in your case. I hired a private investigator to track down evidence I couldn't get any other way. Licensed private investigators (many are former cops) have access to programs and systems the public doesn't, and the information they obtain can be invaluable, even if all you are doing is trying to force your spouse to settle fairly with you. These professionals aren't as pricy as attorneys, but the expense can be significant, so be a smart shopper and find the best one you can afford.

I talked about restraining orders earlier, and they can come into play at any time during the process of your divorce—any time you don't feel safe. In an emergency situation, a law-enforcement officer can ask a judge to sign an emergency restraining order, even if the court is closed.[10] But if the responding officer doesn't feel your situation requires an emergency restraining order, you can still request one at your local courthouse during business hours by filling out the appropriate paperwork. If all that paperwork intimidates you, there are programs that assist victims with this. Speak to someone at a local women's shelter or victim assistance program, typically located in the police department.

Once you've gone through this process, your restraining order will involve some court hearings where you will testify about the abuse you've suffered. You'll want to prepare what you intend to say and be ready to provide specifics: dates, times, scenarios. You'll also want to have copies of any relevant medical and police reports.

As a woman who was given a one-month restraining order that was continually rolled forward, I implore you to keep track of your documents. It will be your job, as your order expires, to stand up and ask the judge, "Who will prepare the restraining court order to extend the expiration?" Whether the answer is your attorney, the courthouse clerks, or the other party's attorney, you must follow up! Push your attorney to draft the order and send it to you so you have a chance to review or edit it before it is filed. Make sure the document is submitted to and signed by the family court judge. Be aware, though, that it may take days or weeks after a court hearing for the order to be submitted and signed by a judge.

Many advocates recommend keeping a printed copy of each court order in your purse, car, and house, but this can be difficult when multiple orders are involved. In my case, it made me feel physically burdened by my proceedings. You have the option of storing your documents electronically on a Google drive, or saved in your iCloud files. Whatever you decide to do, save your documents carefully and keep them accessible to you and you alone. Whatever it feels like, remember that these orders actually free you from your partner's control.

Before we leave the subject of the law, I want to give you a little pep talk. I understand that many women facings a divorce after (or in the midst of) abuse feel weak. They certainly don't feel strong enough to go through the literal trials of a court action. If this describes you, I want to assure you that you will find the strength—especially once you have found good legal allies who can walk you through the process, answer your questions, and fight for you as they are paid to do.

There is no way I can cover all of the details involved in family court proceedings—that would fill a whole book in itself—and it's not the book I set out to write. But I hope I've answered some of your questions here and given you a foundation in the process so that you can move ahead and take action.

You are reading this because you are ready to change your life. This is your chance to do it, so don't turn back! Don't become a deadly statistic. Don't reach out to your abusive partner for reconciliation or even closure. You will not be able to find the closure you seek. Instead, focus on yourself and strive to break your "habit," just as if your relationship with him were an addiction—because in some ways, it is. The symptoms of your "withdrawal" will be similar to addiction too: fatigue, anxiety, depression, maybe even panic attacks.

There's no getting around it; family court proceedings can be tough to endure. But you will get through the process and be better off on the other side. Trust me on that.

Chapter 8

Revival

"Believe you can and you're halfway there."
—THEODORE ROOSEVELT

The key to your survival is adaptability. Your life is changing fast—probably faster than you can keep up with. Who are you, the Kardashians? Try to avoid relying on preconceived notions of how your new life should pan out. Both you and your kids are going to have to adjust to your new living situation, and there is no set timeline for that. Think of it this way: it took you a long time to build the life you left, and it will take you a long time to build a new one. Since you are on your own this time, it could take even longer to feel that your "new normal" really *is* normal.

One thing is for sure: you will never be the same. The experience of leaving a marriage has changed you; now there is no going back. Anyway, why would you want to? Without even knowing you, I know that you are stronger, braver, and smarter than you were when you sat at your old kitchen table or tossed and turned at night, worrying and crying about your imperfect life and how to extricate yourself from it.

All of that said, you do need to take concrete steps to begin your new life. Number one, especially if you have children, is to create a stable home with order, rules, and routines. Life may be different than it was, but it doesn't have to be chaotic. On the contrary, now that one big X factor is gone—an unpredictable, dangerous, or difficult spouse—your home life can be more peaceful, productive, and, yes, happier than ever.

Try to eat dinner at the same time every day, and meals should be prepared ahead of time. Maybe you want to make each Friday "Pizza Night," or initiate "Taco Tuesday." Food doesn't have to be fancy to be satisfying, and mealtime, especially dinnertime, is very important for all of you. It's a great time to have conversations about feelings and fears. It's also important to keep up with what your children are experiencing at school and with their friends. You may be going through a lot yourself, but don't take your eye off the ball when it comes to your kids' needs. Are they keeping up with their schoolwork? Depression can get in the way of that, so monitor it closely and speak with their teachers often. Are they being bullied or teased about the divorce (or anything else)? This can be serious and have dire consequences.

Intervene actively if you think your kids are being threatened or harmed by other kids, including online bullying.

Meanwhile, you have to take care of yourself too. You can't be an effective parent if you aren't functioning at full capacity, so make sure you aren't allowing yourself to get pulled under by depression. Seek help from a pastor, counselor, support group, psychologist, or psychiatrist if you need it.

The bottom line is this: no one else can or will take care of you like you can, so think about what might help you pull yourself out of the misery of fear and anxiety. A divorce can challenge your sense of who you are and what you are worth. Self-esteem comes from within, so dig deep, and remember to lean on those helpers I mentioned above. There is no shame in therapy or support groups. Three important disciplines I implemented when I was starting my new life proved to be key factors in my endurance, both emotional and physical: get healthy, get active, and pamper yourself.

- **Get healthy.** Taking care of your body is essential in being your best self. Maybe all of that late-night worrying has been accompanied by raids in the refrigerator. Maybe you've put on a few pounds and feel ashamed of your body. Don't worry about it; instead, do something! Make a diet plan that includes healthier food choices and stop all that snacking. Getting back on track nutritionally will make you feel more in control of your life, give you more endurance for the challenges you face, and make you feel better about yourself.

· **Get active.** Smart eating alone won't get you to your goal. You need to start moving too. If you don't want to join a gym, there are plenty of workouts you can do at home. Or put on some loud music and dance around your living room. With nothing but a decent pair of sneakers, you can get outside and walk or run around the block, around the neighborhood, or around town. Don't overdo it at first, but you'll probably find yourself going farther and faster the longer you stick with it. The best part is getting your heart rate up, your blood pumping, and your sweat flowing, which will help your mood enormously. It's a scientific fact that the endorphins released during exercise elevate your mood. And when you look in the mirror and see a leaner, healthier body, you'll feel even better!

In a study published in 2016, a group of twenty-four women ranging in age from twenty to sixty and diagnosed with Major Depressive Disorder (MDD) were observed doing physical exercise.[11] They were given baseline questionnaires designed to measure their mood, depression, anxiety levels, and perceptions about exercise. They were then observed on four separate days at least a week apart. In each session, they spent the first thirty minutes resting, then engaged in periods of light, moderate, and strenuous exercise on a rowing machine. (Protocols were put in place to make sure the study was fair and accurate.)

After each session, participants were asked to fill out new questionnaires covering some of the same questions they'd answered before the study. It won't surprise you to learn that the researchers concluded that exercise did have an acute antidepressant effect, and the more vigorous the exercise, the more salutary the effect on the women's sense of well-being.

How does this relate to you? The real takeaway from this and many other studies is that simply adding thirty minutes of exercise to your week can improve your mood drastically. If you have time for more than that, even better! The best way to make sure you exercise regularly is to find the kinds of exercise you like, whether it's cycling, Zumba classes, jogging laps around a track, or swimming laps in a pool. Even a vigorous walk, fifteen minutes out and fifteen minutes back, counts.

Don't give up after a week or two. Another study, conducted by the Department of Kinesiology at the University of Georgia, found that six weeks of regular exercise reduced feelings of fatigue for thirty-six healthy people who had reported persistent fatigue.[12]

Many things in your life are changing and may seem hard to control, but your body is yours, and controlling it with a healthy diet and regular physical activity can reestablish feelings of control over your life as a whole. It can also help you release all those painful relationship memories, anger, and bitterness and enable you to become a calmer, happier person, and a more patient parent.

- **Pamper yourself.** Money may be tight right now, and I'm not suggesting that you go out and buy a Mercedes or book a trip to Spain. But if you get creative, you can find ways to indulge yourself that don't cost next month's rent. Get a new haircut, a pedicure, or a facial. Toss out those stretched-out bras and panties and buy some pretty new lingerie, even if you are the only one who will see the upgraded undies. Go through your closets and *purge* all that stuff that is out of style or no longer suits you. Purchase a couple of basic new pieces that work well for day or night. And (here's my favorite) stop in the "athleisure" section and buy some cool new workout clothes. That'll make you feel more like getting after those workouts! When you pamper yourself, you are letting yourself and the world know you deserve to live well. That's why you're starting this new life in the first place, right?

Life is too short to spend years nursing your grudges and pain. Take whatever steps you need to get healthy and strong inside and out so your new life can begin now. Stay busy, but don't overwhelm yourself by planning too many things. Leave some "air" in your schedule to just relax and enjoy your kids and your solitude. Routines are a good thing, but so is breaking out of them once in a while. Every single person has purpose and meaning. Remember this or write it down and tape it to your bathroom mirror: YOU ARE WORTHY OF LOVE.

Chapter 9

Breaking Down Barriers

"Every day you face battles—that is the reality for all creatures in their struggle to survive. But the greatest battle of all is with yourself—your weaknesses, your emotions, your lack of resolution in seeing things through to the end."

—ROBERT GREENE, THE 33 STRATEGIES OF WAR

My own obstacles held me down until I figured out what they were and broke through them. Why was I trying so hard to be with someone who bullied me and made me feel like a terrible wife and mother? What were the barriers to my happiness? I realized these four things were blocking me:

· Fear of hurting my kids

· Fear of going against my Christian beliefs

· Fear of how I would be perceived by society

· Sexual loneliness

Keeping Kids First. Let's take these one at a time, starting with our responsibility to our children. My ex convinced me that if I left him, I would be forcing my kids to be raised without a father. He made me believe this was the worst possible thing a mother could do. This guilt immobilized me and made me feel like any wrong move I made would hurt my children's futures. I know now that there are *so* many things wrong with that idea! First of all, divorced fathers can and should continue to play a role in their children's lives. One of the goals of a "successful" divorce is that no matter how bad things get between parents, they keep the well-being of their kids in mind, and ideally, both parents stay in their kids' lives. It can be hard to work these things out sometimes in the midst of all the anger and bitterness, but it's possible. And if a father walks away from his kids after a divorce, that behavior is his choice. That behavior is on *him.* Yes, raising kids without a father can be hard on them, but whose fault is it? It's absolutely *not* the kids' fault.

There are some fathers who aren't fit to be in their children's lives, but that is another situation entirely, and a deeply sad one. When a parent is abusive toward his child or subjects the child to situations including the abuse of drugs or alcohol, it is in the best interest of kids to get them away from that toxic or dangerous parent. At these times during a hostile separation, you may have to make difficult choices in order to keep your children safe. Whatever the situation, I see now (and I want you to see) that it is a mistake to feel guilty for ending a bad marriage just because you happen to have brought children into the world together. Families don't all look alike, and "intact" families aren't necessarily best for everyone.

What Will God Think? Throughout my divorce journey, I continued to attend church every Sunday, but it became more and more painful week by week. Why? I am a believer committed to Jesus Christ. I still loved the fellowship, the songs, and the pastor's moving and important sermons. So why did attending church suddenly make me feel sad and angry?

When I thought about it, I realized what I was really feeling was jealousy. I was jealous of the young and old couples around me who seemed to have perfect lives—perfect loves—when mine was desperately imperfect. Why wasn't I blessed to have a loving spouse and perfect family too? Had I done something wrong in God's eyes? Had He forsaken me and condemned me to the role of "black sheep" in my community? How did I become the woman at the well—an outcast in a society of outcasts?

I figured I must have done something wrong to be afflicted with the loneliness I felt, even when surrounded by others. Yet deep down, I knew that letting go of my marriage was the right thing to do. I did not deserve the treatment my husband inflicted upon me. Looking back on it, I see that my church family tried their best to support me, and in no way did they try to make me feel the way I did. And God had certainly not turned His back on me. I was simply clouded by the weight of shame and jealously. I had mixed up my duty to God and to my abusive ex-spouse.

If you are a person of faith like I am, then I'm sure you have grappled with God's will in this difficult time, and with your responsibility to Him and to your spouse. I can see now that my duty to bring my spouse closer to Christ did not oblige me to ignore his cruel actions. The anguish, sorrow, and broken hopes that had been shattered by violence and abuse were palpable in the air. But, in the midst of the cloudy divorce process, I was confused. Wasn't my duty as a Christian woman to obey and trust my husband? What if that put me and my kids in harm's way? I desperately wanted to give our marriage a chance, but I was terrified. I was at a loss as to what to do. As a Christian, I cherish forgiveness, I found it impossible to bear the anguish of unforgiveness between us. In a violent relationship, however, forgiving the violence through reconciliation might put the abused spouse (as well as children and family members) in danger. The process of forgiveness demands courage to confront the truth before resentment can be freed. In fact, the reality of abuse frequently means that reconciliation is not feasible for the protection of all people involved.

In desperation, I called my pastor to ask him for help. We talked through my situation. As I poured out my story, I shed many tears, and when I'd said all I had to say, a sense of relief washed over me—even before he responded. Sometimes just talking with a person you trust can help you find your own answers. And in my case, I was fortunate to have a sympathetic and wise man of God to confide in.

"God did not intend you to suffer within a bad relationship, or to keep silent and compliant when someone was hurting you," my pastor reassured me. "See *1 Corinthians 7:15–16 (nlt)* for yourself."

> *"But if the unbeliever husband or wife who isn't a believer insists on leaving, let them go. In such cases the believing husband or wife is no longer bound to the other, for God has called you to live in peace."*
>
> —1 CORINTHIANS 7:15–16 (NLT)

Again, an overwhelming sense of relief washed over me. *God has called you to live in peace. Peace, not regret, shame, or jealously.* At that moment I started to feel at peace with the way my life had changed, and to see it as a new beginning rather than a terrible ending. Forgiveness gave my heart freedom and the capacity to move forward. Of course, I'm not perfect, so I can't say all my feelings of jealousy washed away. But through Scripture, prayer, and reading books, I no longer carry jealousy around with me like a suitcase filled with bricks. Even now, having done everything in my power to save my marriage, I can let it go and know that God is smiling at my strength and fortitude. For all of the new challenges in my life, I can honestly say that I live in peace now.

The Weight of Society. In addition, let's look at my concern about being judged by my fellow men and women. As I began to tell people the news of my impending divorce—and as word began to spread on its own, as "good gossip" always does—I felt subtle changes in the way people behaved toward me, looked at me, and talked to me. No one was cruel, quite the opposite, but I could see their expressions change. Was it sadness? Pity? Were they judging me?

It felt almost as if I were a doctor telling patients' families that their loved one had died, except it was my marriage that was laid out in the morgue. Their reactions made me feel worse than I already did—to the point where I dreaded telling people or seeing someone for the first time after they heard about the divorce. Even the cashier at the breakfast cafe we'd frequented as a married couple was sad to hear the news. I dreaded the question, "What happened?" If people were just being kind, and I believe they were, why did their reactions make me feel as if I'd done something wrong? Why did I feel the need to comfort and reassure *them* that my divorce was for the best?

Maybe because I still thought of my divorce as a failure—my failure. And maybe because I was battling all of those images (in real life, on social media, on TV, and in magazines) of perfect couples and perfect lives. The truth is divorce is shockingly common. I doubt there is anyone in this country who hasn't been touched by it in some way. Two people get married in good faith, but things can and do change. There are a million ways they change for the worse, but there is only one way to end the suffering, and that is by dissolving the marriage. Only God and you know what you have done and how hard you have tried. God is the only one who fully understands and knows the reasons why you made certain choices, so only His opinion matters. And He wants you safe and happy—not beaten down, abused, and miserable. You were not designed to bear the pain of abuse and heartache. Pain and heartache are indicators that something isn't right, and it needs to be addressed. Your pain is not meaningless; it has a purpose. You may not realize it right now, but you will gain knowledge and strength as a result of this difficult season.

Sexual Loneliness. Finally, I believe it is important to mention sex. Since we live in such a sexualized world, it is important to address this issue. As you know, our sexual desire (libido) is fueled by a mix of neurochemicals (dopamine, norepinephrine, and serotonin). Sex is most meaningful, pleasurable, and fulfilling—emotionally safe as well as physically safe—when it occurs within a loving and binding committed relationship. Of course, sex is about much more than the body. It is the emotional or psychological dimension of sex that makes it distinctively human. Our entire person—mind, body, and soul—is involved. That's why sexual intimacy has potentially powerful emotional consequences. The media doesn't depict the emotional consequences of sex; indeed, television and the movies typically depict sex as consequence-free.

After a painful breakup, you may feel the urge to fill that sexual void. Sex has the potential to cause deeper wounds and pain. As I previously mentioned, sex activates many chemical reactions in our bodies and can quickly become addictive. There is much to be said about the risks of pregnancy and sexually transmitted infections (STIs) from one-night stands—but far less about the emotional hazards. The destructive psychological consequences of temporary sexual relationships may have very negative consequences or effects. Sex can drive a lonely person into madness. Some of the psychological consequences of sex too soon after trauma are feelings of regret, guilt, shaken trust, and/or damaged/ruined relationships. The solace you seek after a breakup will not come from a random one-night stand. It will lead you into disappointment and despair. Emotional repercussions of sexual experiences too soon after a breakup should not be taken lightly. A brief moment of reflection reminds us that emotional issues can have negative, even crippling, consequences for a person's ability to live a happy and productive life.

It may seem like a social norm to jump back into the dating world. You may fulfill a short-term sexual gratification in lieu of your spiritual harmony. I realize this is a provocative statement; however, I have found success by remaining abstinent. I recognize this seems like an extreme idea. I have been torn myself on whether I should include this message in this book. I have learned trying to replace or fill the hollow cavity in your heart through sex will not bring you happiness. Abstinence has allowed me to learn patience and wisdom while I rebuild my life.

Christianity teaches that sex is a beautiful gift from God, but God reserves sex for the committed, loving relationship that only a marriage can provide. But what happens when that marriage has ended in divorce? Before you can love someone, you must first learn to love yourself. You will not find healing in man alone. You don't want to be burned again, and that's understandable. You can't change the past, but you can choose the decisions you make for the future. You can make a fresh start. It's not too late, no matter what your age. You have the freedom at any point in your life to make different choices.

It's important to understand—*deep down*—that your divorce doesn't define you. It is not the sum total of who you are. There are those who will judge you, but you do not have to feel judged. So, stop thinking about *them*! The people who are worth keeping in your life will treat you with compassion and respect.

Now that we have examined the barriers to post-divorce happiness, do you see how we have pushed them aside (or at least made huge cracks in them)? When I set out to write this book, I wanted to share whatever tools I'd found along my journey that might help you move forward as I have. Understand that the process isn't linear; sometimes it's one step forward and two steps back. Remind yourself that it's okay. Sometimes it is *ten* steps forward and a nice bubble bath at the end of the day!

Maybe you are tired of hearing this, but go easy on yourself. As you look toward the future, take it slowly. Start by making a plan to get through the day, then move on to the week, the month, and eventually the wider future. Control what you feel you can, and eventually your entire life will feel more manageable.

Try to determine what the barriers are to your happiness, then chip away at them by examining and understanding them for what they are. You'll probably see that they aren't really barriers at all, just as I did. There's a quote I often tell myself to help me stay on track emotionally "Just because the past didn't turn out like you wanted it to doesn't mean your future can't be better than you imagined." It is an anonymous quote, but I like to think it was spoken by someone who knew what it meant to overcome the challenge of change.

Chapter 10

Healing: Five Essential Steps

"Your attitude, not your aptitude, will determine your altitude."

—ZIG ZIGLAR

I made a conscious decision to cover a lot of ground in this book—from the legal and technical aspects of divorce to the deeply personal ones. There are other books out there that tackle specific elements in depth, and I encourage you to find the ones you need. My mission is to provide you with an overview—sort of like a drone flying *over* a wide area so you can get the "lay of the land" and equip yourself to touch down safely. In this chapter and the next, I go over steps you must take toward that safe landing and a healthy future.

You may be aware of the twelve-step program associated with Alcoholics Anonymous. Members of AA are encouraged to follow each of the twelve steps, working them in order and skipping over none of them, no matter how hard they might be, in order to achieve and maintain sobriety. My roadmap for a healthy life after divorce is easier! I offer you just five essential steps. My hope is that you reap the benefits of following them, just as I have. I struggled a bit with the order here, so consider that part flexible.

Grieve. Divorce isn't death, but it is an end of sorts. A loss. Mourn it. Both you and your kids have lost your family as it once was, and it makes sense to grieve. This is true no matter who ended the marriage. It is true even if you are relieved it's over and you understand it's for the best. When your kids come to you asking whether Daddy is ever coming back—wondering why you can't all be an intact family again—you must be patient and help them understand that some losses are permanent. Some changes are necessary. They will feel better soon, even if it doesn't seem like it right now. Life will be normal again, even if it is a *new* normal. As you convince them of these things, you will convince yourself too. All of this may unleash strong feelings of grief, and that is perfectly natural.

Slow Down. If your marriage was bad for a long time, you may feel impatient to get into a new and better relationship. You may feel you are ready for it, and you don't want to waste any more time feeling sad and alone. I would urge you to proceed with caution. Grief has no timetable; it is different for each person and family. If you are concerned that you might be rushing into something, you probably are. Before you can bring your best self to a new relationship, several things must be true.

- **You must become self-sufficient, independent, and in control of your life.** A relationship started on the basis of *need* (i.e., "I *need* a man in my life) is unlikely to thrive. The best relationships come together out of desire, mutual respect, and interest, not hardship.

- **You must feel certain that your kids are okay.** If you get involved with someone new before your kids are ready to deal with sharing you (and with seeing their father "replaced"), you will carry a heavy burden of guilt into that new relationship. *Take your time and put your children first!* The more time you give them to get used to their new reality, the easier it will be for *all* of you to welcome someone new into the equation.

- **You must be ready. Really ready.** Learn from this toxic relationship. Be able to identify red flags, or warning signs. Get smarter from this situation. Nobody can tell you when you are really ready to venture into another relationship, but deep down you'll know. You'll know because the thought of it will calm you, not stir you up. It won't feel as if you are escaping from your old life; more like you are stepping gracefully into a new one. When you're ready, your judgment will be better, and you'll be much more likely to get serious about someone who is genuinely good for you and your children. Remember, not every guy you go out with will be a potential Mr. Right. You might want to go on some friendly, casual dates and take it very s-l-o-w-l-y for a while. Dating is a whole other world, and even casual dates require that you and your family be ready. Really ready.

Reflect. Healing isn't just a waiting game. It involves introspection and reflection too. You may feel you've made some mistakes, but trust me, every day will bring you a new chance to try things differently. Without dwelling on the past, think about both the good and bad aspects of your marriage, what your hopes for it were and where it went off the rails. It may appear that there were more bad days than happy days during the marriage. Give yourself credit for emerging from it strong and positive, and think about what you can change about yourself so that you are never in that situation again. I guess I don't have to tell you that books can be helpful, since you are reading one now! Read all kinds of books—even novels—and watch all kinds of movies on the topic of divorce. The more stories you hear, true or imagined, the less alone you will feel, and the more you will learn. Avail yourself of the collective wisdom out there. Toward the end of this book, I recommend a list of books and movies I found helpful as I processed my own divorce.

Rely on trusted friends. Sometimes the best help comes from those who care enough about us to listen and respond honestly and with love. Find a family member or friend you can vent to, cry to, and bounce ideas off. Tell that person that in addition to moral support, you want him or her to challenge you. If your confidence is lapsing into self-pity, blame, or bitterness, that person should tell you so. A shoulder is important, but so is honesty.

Seek therapy if you need it—and you probably do. If you had a persistent stomachache, you wouldn't think twice about going to your doctor. The persistent pain of divorce is just another kind of problem that may call for the help of a trained expert. Whether you go to a pastor, psychologist, social worker, or other type of counselor—or join a facilitated support group—there is a lot of value in talking to a professional. Set clear goals, find the right person, and remember that your therapeutic journey doesn't have to be a long one. Also, consider family therapy for both you and your children. Never feel guilty about needing the help of a therapist or counselor. Separating and/or divorcing from an abusive or substance-abusive partner is a marathon, not a sprint.

Retrain Your Brain. At this point, I'd like to focus on the physical aspect of experiencing a traumatic event or a series of events. A traumatic experience can result in long-term anxiety issues, manifested as emotional and/or physiological problems. This anxiety caused by trauma will progress to a more severe condition known as post-traumatic stress disorder (PTSD). Being subjected to traumatic events, such as sexual harassment or a violent crime, or witnessing abuse or fighting, increases the probability of developing PTSD. The Diagnostic and Statistical Manual of Mental Health Conditions is the definitive document that health care providers and researchers use to help diagnose PTSD and other mental health disorders (DSM). This text describes how each of four symptom clusters can trigger unique reactions in response to a traumatic incident: interference of reoccurring memories of the event, avoidance, mood and cognition shifts, and hyperarousal. Long-term effects of PTSD include troubling flashbacks, insomnia, hyperarousal, and anxiety, which may cause severe disability. Researchers from Uppsala University and Karolinska Institute published a study that found that people with PTSD have an imbalance between two essential neurochemical systems in the brain: (1) serotonin and (2) substance P.[13] PET scanners were used to test the interaction between the two brain signaling systems. In sixteen patients with PTSD and sixteen healthy controls, researchers looked at the serotonin and substance P/neurokinin-1 (SP/NK1) systems separately as well as their overlapping expression.

According to the findings, the greater the imbalance between these chemicals, the more serious the patients' PTSD symptoms demonstrate. Both of these neuro-chemical processes have been related to stress and anxiety on their own, but their interactions may be critical in human anxiety disorders.

With this knowledge in mind, you may be affected by a mental health issue. You may have to recognize there has been a chemical imbalance affecting you physically. There is a plethora of therapies covered in the next chapter. Yet, even after all of the grieving and reflection, your mind may continue to travel to dark places. Late at night, when the kids are asleep and you are tossing and turning, you may find yourself reliving old arguments with your ex or revisiting the rage you felt when he let you down. To break free of the thoughts that weigh on you, you may need to retrain your brain. And like all training, that involves exercise.

I have found two effective strategies to retrain your brain: distraction and intentional application.

Distraction. Listen to music or audio books, pray, meditate, watch a funny cat video, or play a game on your phone. Don't worry about "wasting time." Mindless or passive activities can help you break free of bad thought patterns or painful memories. Get in the habit of redirecting your thoughts using any distractions that work. And if that involves getting up in the middle of the night and watching reruns of old TV shows, so be it. Don't be surprised if you hear yourself laughing out loud.

Intentional application. Purposely focus your intellect on searching for your answers through spiritual faith. As a Christian, when I am hurting and lost, I can always find footing in reading my Bible. On occasion, I search the "life choices" index in the back to find answers to my questions. I realize this may not be everyone's path; nevertheless, I feel the urge to share this part of my faith with you. The following verses from Scripture have helped me time and again:

> "The Lord is near to the brokenhearted and saves the crushed in spirit"
> —PSALM 34:18 (ESV)

> "Then Jesus said, "Come to me, all of you who are weary and carry heavy burdens, and I will give you rest"
> —MATTHEW 11:28 NLT

The physical pain you may be feeling in this moment in your life is real. It hurts. These strategies take practice in a time where there is no time. They aren't a cure for PTSD. However, they are avenues on your road map to rebuilding your life.

Which brings me to the last essential step on my list:

Learn to Laugh Again. It's a cliché to say that laughter is the best medicine, but like most clichés, it happens to be true. Studies have shown that laughter stimulates the endorphins or "feel good" chemicals in your body.[14] This is a blessing because you've just been through a period where you didn't feel much like laughing, and now you are probably overdue for a healing dose.

Don't believe me? During a 2016 meeting at the American College of Cardiology, Michael Miller, M.D., of the University of Maryland, reported that in a study of twenty healthy people, laughter did as much good for their arteries as aerobic activity.[15] He wasn't recommending we replace exercise with laughter; he simply suggested we add it to our regimen. "Thirty minutes of exercise three times a week and fifteen minutes of laughter on a daily basis is probably good for the vascular system," he concluded.

This study and various others confirm what you probably sense intuitively. Smiling and laughing elevate our mood and make us feel better all over, creating a snowball effect. The more we smile and laugh, the happier we feel and the more we *feel* like smiling and laughing. Plus, laughter is contagious (which is why TV sitcoms use laugh tracks), so even as you are helping yourself with your LOLs, you're probably "infecting" those around you, including your kids.

So, what makes you laugh? The movies *The Hangover* and *The First Wives Club* do the trick for me, but maybe your taste runs more toward funny pet TikTok videos. Cable TV and digital streaming media such as YouTube, Netflix, and Hulu are filled with sitcoms, TV series, standup comedy performances, and other offerings designed to send us into spasms of laughter. Allow yourself some guilt-free time to indulge in stories, humor, and pure entertainment.

Playing video and board games with your kids can evoke squeals of laughter from everybody, so find some fun and funny activities you can all do together. You don't need to understand the science behind laughter to derive benefit from it; trust me, though, the science is there. As you laugh, hormones flood into your bloodstream and your arteries dilate. This provides a surge of good feelings, improving your mood and releasing pain and tension throughout your body. This release can stave off depression as well as all the anger and frustration that built up during your divorce journey.

Life is too short not to laugh, and laughter involves letting go. The Zig Ziglar quote at the opening of this chapter states, "Your attitude, not your aptitude, will determine your altitude." What does this really mean? To me, it's how we respond to life in a manner that allows us to accept the duality, the contradictions around us. A positive attitude, even if we have not yet mastered things in our life, enables us to make a difference in our personal circle (family, friends) and extended circle (community, world) so we can be change agents for higher living. This "altitude" that Ziglar refers to is a powerful state of being in which you are not easily knocked down by the negative circumstances around you. So let go of blame, anger, and sadness and embrace all that is rich and enjoyable (including humor) in life. If you figure out how to laugh when you'd rather yell or cry, then you will soon feel like laughing more often. Life is too short to hold on to the past.

Reread the five basic steps and all that goes with them as necessary. A better life awaits, once you:

- Grieve
- Slow Down
- Reflect
- Retrain Your Brain
- Learn to Laugh Again

Chapter 11

Take Back Control

"If you're going through hell, keep going."
—WINSTON CHURCHILL

Once you have separated from your ex, you'll need to identify what emotions your body is experiencing. This process is what will get you through your trauma and encourage you to take back control of your life. *The Body Keeps the Score*, by Bessel van der Kolk, is a book I recommend that will help you understand the many ways trauma has attached itself to your body, not just to your emotions. When you have been in a heightened state of fear or unrest in your marriage for years, your body might have developed some chronic (but treatable) ailments, such as back pain, migraines, digestive issues, irritable bowl, chronic fatigue, and a host of other bodily upsets. By identifying your trauma, then working through it through various practices that a counselor can suggest, it is possible to find healing.

As I mentioned in chapter ten, finding the right kind of counselor who aligns with your personality and your belief system is key to this process. Seeking clinical help doesn't mean you have a mental disorder; it just means you are admitting that your problems are too large to easily handle on your own.

There are many avenues for finding the right counselor. If money is an issue, you can search within your insurance network. If you are a student, your school probably offers counseling through student health services. If you're a member of a religious congregation, you can begin by speaking to your pastor, priest, rabbi, or religious leader. And if none of those is viable for you, your local police department typically offer free counseling services for victims of a crime. Shelters that harbor abused women and children offer free counseling too.

In addition to the help you get from professionals, there's a lot you can do to help yourself take back control. As you navigate your way through either family or criminal court, you may find yourself weighed down with court documents and orders. Keep your court documents organized, but always leave them at home. Don't drag them along like a symbol of your pain. Keep your restraining orders digital so you don't have to worry about carrying a piece of paper with your everywhere you go. Doing so will allow you to live your life unencumbered.

Meditation is another practice I want to bring to your attention. During a divorce, the mind and body are continuously slammed with rage, sadness, fear, anxiety, and depression. I watched helplessly as my skin aged, my hair whitened, my soul grew tired, and my mind became a roller coaster of torturous memories. I searched for answers in books, among my fellow divorcees, and from my counselor. When he suggested meditation for about the tenth time, I finally listened and decided to try it. I figured I had nothing to lose. After practicing a few times, I was unexpectedly surprised at the benefits! Setting aside those few minutes every day to walk myself through a calming and centering series of mental exercises helped me so much that I still meditate at least a few times a week.

So, what exactly *is* it? Meditation is a practice of awareness and mindfulness that allows you to obtain a healthy perspective of your thoughts, feelings, and state of being. It also allows you to be an observer of your thoughts instead of one who judges them. For the basics, you might want to start with the site Mindful.org, which states, "Meditation begins and ends in the body. It involves taking the time to pay attention to where we are and what's going on, and that starts with being aware of our body . . . Your head doesn't become vacuumed free of thought, utterly undistracted. It's a special place where each and every moment is momentous." [16]

According to the renowned author and practitioner Jon Kabat-Zinn, meditation entails "the basic human ability to be fully present, aware of where we are and what we're doing, and not overly reactive or overwhelmed by what's going on around us." [17] In his book *Wherever You Go, There You Are*, Kabat-Zinn says, "You can't stop the waves, but you can learn to surf." This is such a simple thought, but it's so transformative. We can learn to ride the waves of rage and pain rather than being pulled under by them.

The great thing about meditation is that it is totally "portable." It can be practiced anywhere, anytime: at bedtime, in the bathroom, in a halted car, or in a hot tub. It takes some guidance at first, but I can promise you that it will change your perspective about everything in your life.

YouTube has many videos to help you form your personal meditation practice. Two of my favorites are Michael Sealy's "Guided Body Scan Meditation for Mind and Body Healing" and Kabat-Zinn's "Guided Mindfulness Meditation, Series 1, Sitting Meditation." [18] Start there, and then do some exploring.

A little more "out there" but quite useful is float therapy. This is also called restrictive environmental stimulation therapy (REST), and for good reason! With this form of therapy, you climb into a pod or tank filled with super-buoyant warm water. To facilitate floating and soothe the body, the water is infused with a large amount of Epsom salt. The tank, often referred to as a "sensory deprivation tank," is completely dark and silent. Once enclosed, you simply float as if in the womb or outer space. By cutting off all external stimuli, your body relaxes, and you are alone with your thoughts. I can't express to you what a relief it can be when all pressure—including gravitational—is removed. Pain, both psychological and physical, can melt away during this therapy. Time becomes meaningless. You might even find yourself having mild (but harmless) hallucinations, vivid dreams, or even experiencing enhanced creativity during the session.

In my personal experience, I recall floating in my tank with zero distractions: no sound, sight, or gravity. Because of the sensory deprivation, I felt the literal release of the clouds blocking my mind. I achieved a welcome detachment from my circumstances, which allowed me to work through my emotions, calm myself by seeing life's big picture, and ultimately hit the reset button.

Once I'd opened myself up to meditation and float therapy, I became an "inner-space explorer." I tried journaling, yoga, breath work, and massage therapy. Not one of them was a waste of time, though we all have to choose what feels right for us. Here is a list of other practices that have been recommended to me that you might want to look into:

· Kinesiology Therapy

· Therapeutic Hypnosis

· Journaling

- Pet Therapy

- Cognitive Behavioral Therapy (CBT)

- Eye Movement Desensitization and Reprocessing (EMDR)

- Auricular Acupuncture, and Emotional Freedom Technique tapping (EFT).

Divorce intertwined with domestic violence can cause burnout—a loss of motivation from prolonged periods of physical and mental exhaustion. Feeling overwhelmed, drained, and inadequate are symptoms of burnout. These emotions can lead you down a path of physical illness, anxiety, or depressive disorders. Tools such as counseling, meditation, exercise, and conscious behavior change can help you avoid these outcomes by releasing the anxiety and fear summoned by your traumatic experiences.

It should be clear to you by now that there are many professionals and practices out there to help you on your journey to wellness and wholeness. You are not alone. You are not the first to suffer this kind of life change, and you won't be the last. When you accept what has happened in your past and proactively walk into your future with confidence and faith, you have finally begun to take back control of your life.

Chapter 12

What Not to Do

*"When we forgive we are telling God that we
have faith in Him to fight our injustices. It might not
seem possible when you are standing in a storm, but
when you take the high road you can see farther than
you can now."*

—SHANNON L. ALDER, *THE NARCISSISTIC ABUSE RECOVERY BIBLE*

Throughout this book I have tried to be positive and to
offer an optimistic, can-do perspective on moving forward after divorce entangled with abuse. I have no inten-
tion of contradicting that. But in the spirit of positivity,
I do want to look at a few things you should avoid, or at
least keep to a minimum. Let's call this the don't-do list.

Don't be naive. Maybe you didn't see it coming. Maybe
you were blindsided by your divorce, and the traumas

you have endured left you feeling unstable—as if everything you believed was wrong. Put on your big girl panties and get through it! This is just one chapter in your life. You probably made some mistakes or overlooked some warning signs (most of us do), but now is the time to get smart, wake up, and stop living in the dark. Reframe your experiences in a way that puts you in the driver's seat; learn from them, be grateful for the wisdom you've obtained, and move on. Listen to the advice of your lawyers and clinicians: start looking after your own best interests and those of your kids!

Own up to any mistakes you've made along the way, and vow not to repeat them. Forgive yourself and move along. You're already a better person than you were, and you will continue to get better. Trust me when I tell you that the "red flags" in future relationships will be much more obvious to you than they may have been in the past. And that's a good thing.

Don't be vindictive. This is not *The Avengers*, and you're not Tony Stark, vanquishing alien supervillains. Sure, you have been wronged by your soon-to-be (or now) ex. You've been treated badly and maybe even robbed of your dignity a few times. Now that you have clear vision, you can see that your ex is a jerk, an awful liar . . . whatever you want to call him. Even if you could force him to own up to what he did to you, and it's doubtful you could, he probably wouldn't change. You have seen him for who he is. You won't allow him to hurt you anymore, but you can't stop him from being *him*. Moving on to a better life is the best revenge. He will have to go on living with himself, and trust me, he's a miserable person; however, your future now belongs to only you.

Instead of fantasizing about revenge on your ex, take the high road. Neither family nor criminal court will offer you the peace you seek. Find your own sense of peace. Use your mental energy to thrive and grow. Think about all of the ways you are better off without him. Then take note of all the ways your life is already improving. Focus on rebuilding your life and taking care of your children; focus on the things you *can* control. Let go of everything you *can't* control. Whenever you find your mind wandering to your ex, redirect it toward yourself. You deserve your full attention; he doesn't.

Don't talk to just anyone who will listen. In the last chapter, I spent a lot of time telling you about the benefits of speaking to a counselor or therapist and seeking support from friends and family. That's all fine, but don't overdo it in your attempt to gain support. There's probably a fair amount of drama in your story, and by this point, you probably tell it pretty well. Yet it's unnecessary to release all the details about your terrible ex to everyone you meet. Processing is one thing, but spilling your guts all over the place is another. Use a little judgment and discipline about who you choose to open up to. That way, you won't have to navigate all of the "friendly advice" that comes your way.

People mean well, they really do, but it can be confusing to hear too many opinions. Choose your confidants wisely, and share your thoughts and feelings judiciously. Avoid those who pretend to be impartial; they might be wolves in sheep's clothing, including members of your own family. Sometimes even well-meaning parents are so worried about you being alone that they'll advise you to go back to a bad marriage rather than "make waves." Others are just ignorant about what they say; as a result, their words leave you feeling ashamed or anxious when you need to feel confident and empowered.

I'll say it again: Feel free to reach out to loved ones and professionals for the support you need. But don't let your need to share your story keep you stuck on re-play, unable to move on. Go out with friends and tell them you *don't* want to talk about your divorce for the night. You might find yourself having a carefree evening that helps you heal when you don't rehash your recent troubles. Doesn't that sound like more fun than sitting at a bar, pouring your broken heart out for the millionth time?

Don't succumb to regret. If you find yourself ruminating on thoughts such as, *I never should have married him. I should have seen the red flags from the beginning. I should never have gone back. I should have left sooner*, remind yourself that you are making changes *now*. Life is too short to spend your time looking back and wondering what you coulda/shoulda/woulda done differently.

Be here now! Evolve into a strong person. Divorce wasn't part of the plan, but it happened. The exciting question to ask yourself is: What's next?

If you try to move forward while looking back, you might run smack into something. Keep your eyes facing front. There's a lot out there for you to navigate. Change your course over and over if you have to. You'll have plenty of time in the future to salvage the good memories from the past. Be assured they'll always be there for you. Your kids will often remind you of the "good times." For now, focus on what you are *going to do*, not on what you did or didn't do. Your best life is through the windshield, not in the rearview mirror.

My final "don't" is a little more specific than the rest, but I can't stress it enough:

Don't try to be friends with your ex. It's rare, but there are couples who go through a divorce and end up friends. Don't assume that unusual circumstance is something to be desired, or that you will achieve it if you try. Save your friendship for those who deserve it.

Don't get me wrong. I'm not saying you shouldn't be civil to each other. If you have children, it's important to present a united front for them—to cooperate and be good co-parents. That's different from being friends, though. Kourtney Kardashian may go on vacation with her ex, the father of her children, and his new girlfriend (can you even imagine?), but her life is a reality TV show; yours is the real world.

Since the majority of divorces involve pain on both sides, it can seem admirable to try to heal that pain and salvage some meaning by staying close to one another. Trust me, this almost always ends in fresh feelings of disappointment and bitterness. And it usually creeps in just when you are trying to let those things go. It's alright to be cordial, to be kind, and to be a good co-parent. But don't be friends—even if he wants to.

Chapter 13

Clean Up Your
Social Media

"You can't base your LIFE on other people's expecta-tions."

—STEVIE WONDER

The phrase "social media" was a term barely used ten years ago. If you were getting a divorce then, you would have had many of the usual problems, but how to handle your online life probably wouldn't have been one of them. Welcome to the 21st century, where there are multiple versions of "YOU" floating around out there, including Facebook You, Twitter You, Instagram You, LinkedIn You . . . and maybe more, such "Dating Site" You.

The image you project online may be more important than you realize, especially as you reconfigure your life post-divorce. Are you looking for a new job? Potential employers are bound to check your social media profiles as part of their due diligence. Are you starting to think about dating again? Understand that every guy you meet—through friends, at parties, online, wherever—is likely to check out your various profiles as well.

It isn't all bad, of course. LinkedIn is a great place to list career milestones and accomplishments, show your active interest in your chosen field, network, and post testimonials about your work. Your intelligence and sense of humor (and good looks too, let's face it), as showcased on Facebook and Twitter, may impress potential dates. I'm not saying you should lower your profile on social media or eradicate it. I am suggesting you steer it carefully, so it works for you rather than against you. The first thing to realize is that whatever you do online, people are watching, judging, and drawing conclusions. Once you get that through your head, the rest is logical. Over the two years it took me to go from married to divorced, I learned six valuable lessons about social media.

Remove all photos of your ex from your profiles. Think of this as a cleanse or a detox. Disassociating from him is a strategic correction to the impression you are making on the world. Wash him out of your public life. Do a bit of housecleaning in order to move on emotionally. Start off fresh. Think about it: Do you really want the people in your life to think you are still stuck on your ex? Do you want your new friends to define you as part of a couple? I don't think so.

Unfriend or block your ex's family and friends. Of course, you've blocked your ex, but that's not enough. This may sound harsh, but I assure you it is important to block everyone he is closely associated with, including family, friends, and coworkers. I understand you probably think of some of his friends as your friends too. But you must let some people go in the aftermath of a divorce. Losing people is hard, especially when you've already lost so much. But people do choose sides in a divorce filled with animosity. And some will not side with you when the dust settles. It is human nature. Allowing his posse access to your posts and photos and friend list is arming them with information that may get back to your ex, which could potentially hurt you. What seems harmless, a photo of you holding a beer at a party, for example, could be used against you in a custody hearing. Remember, you are still in a battle; no sense offering ammunition to the enemy. And besides, you want to move on. Swimming around in the same old pond won't help you meet new fish!

Do not post rants about your ex. Whatever you do, stay classy online. If that means asking a friend to take away your phone after the second drink, so be it. We all need outlets for the anger divorce can create inside us, but social media is not that outlet. It's just too public, too permanent, and too hard to take back when you're feeling stronger later. In fact, I'd go so far as to say, don't post *anything* about your ex, good or bad. Why give him the satisfaction? Talk to a friend or therapist. Draw a target with his picture on it and throw darts at it. But don't post anything about your ex! If the urge to vent online is overwhelming, step away from your device and sleep on it. I'm pretty sure your compulsion to air your dirty laundry to the world will pass by morning. Take the high road. You'll be proud of yourself for exercising restraint.

Keep it positive. In addition to avoiding rants about *him*, try to avoid negative posts altogether. To paraphrase what your mother probably told you, "If you can't say something nice online, don't say anything." Even on a bad day, there must be something positive to say—about the weather, your kids' grades, or something moving you saw on TV. If you find a quote that inspires you, share it. Maybe it will help someone else. Something unmistakable happens inside you when you send positivity out into the world. It can help brighten the darkness for a moment and make you realize that things are getting better. Stash the snark and dwell on the positive. You'll be making the internet a better place, as well as your own heart.

Don't be a stalker. I said above that your ex and others may be following your posts. Don't be guilty of the same crime! As tempting as it can be to check up on what your ex is doing, and who he's doing it with, resist the urge. Part of cleansing your life is setting boundaries for yourself as well as for him. Embrace your new life, and avoid wallowing in your old one by steering clear of what's going on in his world. When you feel some stalking coming on, redirect that energy into exercise, prayer, meditation, Netflix, or playing Words with Friends.

If all else fails, there's the "nuclear option":

Take a social media break. This one isn't mandatory, and I know social media can be a lifeline during hard times, but it might be a good idea to take a break from Facebook, Instagram, and the rest. If your divorce is like mine, there are a lot of competing voices in your head, telling you you're a failure, you're not lovable, and you're not *perfect*. Do you really need to see photos of your friends' beautifully cooked meals, glorious vacations, and happy (or so you think) relationships? Everything looks so bright and shiny online, even when it isn't. When you aren't feeling strong and powerful, looking into others' lives can be overwhelming and daunting. Step away from it all! Turn off your social media notifications and focus on *you*.

If it's too hard to go cold turkey, designate certain days as free from social media. You'll be amazed at how much more time you have for other things, including real-life encounters with friends and loved ones. And when you do go back, you'll realize you haven't missed a thing. Trust me, less scrolling equals more happiness—at least in the pivotal period of post-divorce adjustment.

Chapter 14

To-Do Lists

"Above all, be the heroine of your life, not the victim."

—NORA EPHRON

I know I've thrown a lot of information your way at a time when it might be hard to absorb it all. Believe me, I understand. I've been there. I hope you'll think of this book not as a lecture but as a supportive reference you can return to when you need it, or when you want help with specific issues. Specifics are important, not just vague ideas. In that spirit, I've included some lists you might find useful. I hope you'll think of them as a jumping-off point and add your own line items. Most important to remember is that it takes a tremendous amount of strength to endure a divorce filled with domestic violence. I hope this book—and my experiences—have resonated with you and brought you some of that strength, along with some comfort and tangible help.

Things Every Divorcing Woman Should Have

1. **Comfy new pillow:** Reward yourself with a new, comfortable pillow. Finally, look forward to a restful night's sleep. You might also want to try a weighted blanket.

2. **Trusted friends:** This one is self-explanatory. The comfort and safety of friends will buffer any turbulence you encounter with your ex.

3. **Journals:** You might want to keep two separate journals: one for important information about your divorce proceedings and questions for your attorney, and one for more general thoughts, prayers, dreams, and feelings. There is nothing like jotting a few honest lines in a journal before bed to help clear your head and prepare for sound sleep.

4. **A good attorney:** We've been over this, but I'll remind you that this is not an area where you can afford to cut corners! If you needed surgery, you'd want the best doctor for the job. Divorce is a kind of surgery, too, so get a second and third opinion before proceeding.

5. **A new perfume:** A new you calls for a new scent!

6. **New undies:** Even if you are the only one who will see them, a pretty new bra and panties will make you feel powerful. Toss out those old things with the sprung elastic and stock up on some high-quality or comfy lingerie.

7. **A new pair of comfortable and chic high heels and a good purse:** It may not be practical to purchase a whole new wardrobe, but great shoes and a smart bag will go a *long* way toward making you look and feel polished and professional at job interviews, on dates, and in court.

8. **A diffuser with essential oils for aromatherapy:** Lavender is calming; citrus is energizing; bergamot alleviates stress . . . and the list goes on. For just a few dollars, you can unleash the power of aromatherapy and make your surroundings more inviting and invigorating. You're worth it!

Goals

My goals are not your goals; therefore, I'm not going to tell you what yours should be. But goals help us move forward, so making a list of your personal/career goals should be a priority right now. Here are some steps you can take to advance your goals. One day you will look back on your life and take inventory of all your amazing accomplishments.

Take new family pictures. Mark this new time in your life with beautiful photos to keep forever, and then think about where you'll be in ten years when you look back at them. For the sake of personal growth, be sure to take some of just *you*, as well as your family and kids.

Re-examine your and career path. Are you on a career path right now, or are just working to make ends meet? Are you in the profession of your dreams, or have you continually put that off? How can you move toward work that is meaningful as well as lucrative? Think about all of these things and start to compile a list of professional goals. Don't be afraid to think big!

Get proactive about improving your health and fitness. Do you have the body and good health you want? Are you taking steps to stay vital and active and fit—for the sake of your kids as well as yourself? What could you do right now to improve this aspect of your life? Compile a list of health and fitness goals, but *be realistic.* Rome wasn't built in a day. Take it step by step, think long-term, and don't beat yourself up if you have some setbacks. Every day is a new opportunity to be healthy.

Review your finances. Are you in debt? Just scraping by each month? Do you have a solid budget you can stick to? A divorce can be hard on a woman's finances, and so can navigating the bills and obligations on your own. Make a list of your monthly expenses and another list of your income. Then come up with ways you can make sure your financial life is solid and healthy. Think about improvements you hope to make in your life and how you can make those happen. You'll have to set priorities and think long-term, but you'll sleep much better if you map out your finances rather than wandering around in the dark. Check out Dave Ramsey's practical baby step plan; it has helped millions of families get rid of debt and change their lives forever. Dave's seven-step plan taught me how to organize my finances and become financially independent.

Those are the basic practicalities, but I urge you to think bigger than the basics. Below are some lists for continued growth. Remember: if you don't dream it, you won't accomplish it!

- Research places you'd like to travel to. And then start budgeting to go there.

- Tackle a new language online, or study a new skill. There's a host of topics to choose from, such as cooking, painting, photography, knitting, writing, or gardening, to name a few.

- Create a recipe file of new dishes you'd like to make. When you have the time and energy, have fun cooking and sharing the meals with your friends and children.

- Investigate new skills you'd like to acquire, from changing a flat tire to repairing a toilet, to driving a standard-transmission car. Think about all of the things you used to rely on your ex to do, then realize you can do every one of them with a little knowledge and effort!

- Find a new hobby. Many communities provide free or lost cost classes such as Zumba, art classes, fitness programs, and so on.

And finally, here's a to-do list from me. These are things I believe will help you move forward. Don't worry about getting them all done instantly. But it does feel good to cross something off your list once it is accomplished. And, again, this is just a start. Please add to my list and personalize it to help you achieve your own goals.

Lydia's To-Do List for Divorcing Women

Rejuvenate your house. Change up your living space and refashion your home into a place of peace and welcoming comfort. This doesn't have to involve an expensive makeover. Choose a new color and paint your walls. Rearrange your furniture, and purchase some throw pillows and a few other pretty accessories. These simple but effective changes can go a long way toward freshening your living space.

Minimize. Pack up any items your ex left behind, as well as things that offer painful reminders of your former life. Let his attorney know when he can pick up his stuff, then arrange to give the rest away, sell it, or toss it. None of this has to involve prolonged interactions with him. Work it out to keep contact to a minimum. If you can't avoid an encounter with him, invite a friend over for moral support (or a police officer, if that's where things stand).

Change your locks. This may seem like overkill, but if you are still living in your marital residence and your ex has keys, you'll never feel truly safe until you know he is locked out for good. You might want to install a surveillance camera or "smart doorbell." They are quite common now and not as expensive as you think.

Invest in a good tool kit and learn how to use everything in it. Now that you're on your own, you'll need to learn how to make small repairs. No need to call a plumber when the toilet is running; there's an easy fix for that if you know how to do it and have the equipment on hand. Check out the tutorials online for every kind of home repair. There's usually an easy-to-follow video for every type of repair. Bonus tip: A toilet can sometimes be unclogged with dish soap. Just pour some in, let it stand for thirty minutes, then try flushing.

Learn how to turn off the power and the main water line to your home. Examine your air filters and make a note to change them out every few months. Have your home inspected for pests—mice, termites, spiders, and such. Keeping up with these little things will prevent you from feeling overwhelmed by solo home ownership. You are stronger and smarter than you think, so act like it!

Recommended List of Books

The Subtle Art of Not Giving a Fuck by Mark Manson

Becoming a Narcissist's Nightmare by Shahida Arabi

33 Strategies of War by Robert Greene

Who Moved My Cheese? by Spencer Johnson

The Total Money Makeover by Dave Ramsey

Enemies of the Heart by Andy Stanley

The Narcissist's Playbook by Dana Morningstar

Wherever You Go, There You Are by Dr. Jon Kabat-Zinn

The Body Keeps the Score by Bessel van der Kolk

Surviving & Thriving after Narcissistic Abuse by Shahida Arabi

The Narcissistic Abuse Recovery Bible by Shannon L. Alder

Lydia's Recommended List of Movies

Want a good laugh? Take your mind off your own drama and watch these recommended lists of movies and television shows—for both a good laugh and a good cry. Movies are a great way to detach your mind from a tough day.

- *Waiting to Exhale*
- *Forgetting Sarah Marshall*
- *Someone Great*
- *The First Wives Club*

Lydia's Recommended List of TV Shows

- *Workin' Moms*
- *Girlfriends Guide to Divorce*
- *Dead to Me*
- *Frank and Grace*
- *Sweet Magnolias*
- *Firefly Lane*

Chapter 15

The Best Is Yet to Come

"At the end of the day, you can either focus on what's tearing you apart or what's keeping you together."

−ANONYMOUS

When I sat down to write this book, it seemed like a huge task to accomplish, and I couldn't imagine ever finishing it. But now that it is almost done, I'm reluctant to end it. I don't want to walk away from you while you are still in pain. I want to continue to reassure you that no matter what has happened, no matter how scared or angry or confused you feel, everything is going to be okay. The fact that I am here telling you so is evidence that it's true!

Whether or not you believe it, you are worthy of love. And self-love is where it begins. Your mindset matters, so it's important to stick to your routines. Build a meaningful life day by day, be disciplined but flexible, think positive, and stay focused. Understand that no matter what you do, divorce is hard work, especially if you had an abusive partner. Acknowledge your hardships, and be proud of every accomplishment. Focus on gratitude as much as you can, and allow yourself to wallow in self-pity every once in a while. Your pain—both psychological and physical—is actually a survival mechanism. It's your body's way of telling you to avoid what caused it. Learn from your pain, but don't let it make your heart hard or cold. Use it to become stronger, smarter, and more compassionate toward yourself and others. Your heart did not break overnight, and it will not heal overnight either. You cannot overcome the impacts of years of trauma in one second. Give yourself the room to heal and grow.

I have spent an entire book urging you to move on, but that doesn't mean you should forget your past; it's a crucial part of your story. Take everything you've learned from the past and use it to construct your new life. Your book has many chapters waiting to be revealed. Don't be afraid to turn the page!

Resources

Address Confidentiality

Address Confidentiality Programs were created to protect victims of stalking, domestic violence, sexual assault, and other crimes from offenders who use public records, such as voter or drivers' license registries, to locate them. These programs give victims a legal substitute address (usually a post office box) to use in place of their physical address. This address can be used whenever an address is required by public agencies. First class mail sent to the substitute address is forwarded to the victim's actual address. and links, or connect to data from your collection.

https://victimconnect.org/resources/address-confidentiality/

Angel Flight West

Provides relocation flights for Domestic violence survivors, shelter to shelter. To help survivors start a new life in another city, but cannot afford to leave.

www.angelflightwest.org

Crime Victim Compensation

Every state has a crime victim or criminal injuries compensation program to help pay some of the out-of-pocket expenses for victims of crime. Most programs are limited to victims of violent crimes, but some programs will also pay the counseling costs for victims of major financial crimes. Every state sets limits on the overall amount that can be paid to a victim and on the amount paid for each type of expense. Victim compensation only pays where there is not insurance coverage or some other type of payment available.

Find your state's crime victim compensation program through the National Association of Crime Victim Compensation Boards.

https://nacvcb.org

DOD Safe Helpline for Sexual Assault

The Department of Defense (DOD) Safe Helpline is a crisis support service designed to provide sexual assault services for survivors, their loved ones, and other members of the DOD community. Available 24 hours a day, 7 days a week via phone and online chat.

Hotline: 1 (877) 995–5247

https://safehelpline.org

Human Trafficking

The National Human Trafficking Hotline is a national anti-trafficking hotline serving victims and survivors of human trafficking and the anti-trafficking community in the United States. The toll-free hotline is available to answer calls from anywhere in the country, 24 hours a day, 7 days a week, every day of the year in more than 200 languages.

Hotline: 1 (888) 373-7888 | Text: 233733

https://humantraffickinghotline.org

Legal Aid Society

Legal aid handles cases involving Domestic violence– legal aid can help you obtain a protective order, a child custody order and divorce.

https://www.lawhelp.org/find-help/

National Domestic Violence Hotline

Services are always free and available 24/7. Advocates are available to listen without judgement and help you begin to address what's going on in your relationship.

Hotline: 1 (800) 799-7233

https://www.thehotline.org

National Teen Dating Abuse

Love is Respect offers information, support, and advocacy to young people who have questions or concerns about their dating relationships. Available 24 hours a day, 7 days a week via phone, text, and online chat.

Hotline: 1 (866) 331–9474 | Text: 22522

https://www.loveisrespect.org

Veteran Crisis Line

The Veterans Crisis Line will connect you to qualified and caring responders with the Department of Veterans Affairs. This 24/7 lifeline serves all Veterans, Service Members, National Guard, and Reserve and their family members and friends.

Hotline 1 (800) 273-8255 press 1 | Text 838255

https://www.veteranscrisisline.net

Womens Law

The WomensLaw online helpline provides basic legal information, referrals, and emotional support for victims of abuse.

https://www.womenslaw.org

References

1. NCADV: National Coalition Against Domestic Violence. (n.d.). Retrieved August 13, 2020, from https://ncadv.org/get-help.

2. National Domestic Violence Hotline: Get Help Today: 1-800-799-7233. Retrieved August 13, 2020, from https://www.thehotline.org/.

3. Petrosky E, Blair JM, Betz CJ, Fowler KA, Jack SP, Lyons BH. Racial and Ethnic Differences in Homicides of Adult Women and the Role of Intimate Partner Violence—MMWR Morb Mortal Wkly Rep 2017;66:741–746. DOI: http://dx.doi.org/10.15585/mmwr.mm6628a1External.

4. Kippert, A., Fontes, L., Flannery, S., & Jeltsen, M. (n.d.). "Find Domestic Violence and Abuse Help, Information and Stats." Retrieved August 13, 2020, from https://www.domesticshelters.org/.

5. Victim Connect Resource Center. "Address Confidentiality," n.d. https://victimconnect.org/resources/address-confidentiality/.

6. Amy E. Bonomi, Rashmi Gangamma, Chris R. Locke, Heather Katafiasz, David Martin, "Meet me at the hill where we used to park": Interpersonal processes associated with victim recantation, Social Science & Medicine, Volume 73, Issue 7, 2011, Pages 1054-1061, ISSN 0277-9536, https://doi.org/10.1016/j.socscimed.2011.07.005.

7. Domestic Violence/Dating Violence. (2019, October 21). Retrieved August 13, 2020, from https://www.womenslaw.org/about-abuse/forms-abuse/domestic-violencedating-violence.

8. State Side Legal, Pine Tree Legal Assistance, statesidelegal.org/.

9. "2012 Truth About Abuse Survey Report."*org*, Mary Kay Inc., 2012, vawnet.org/material/2012-truth-about-abuse-survey-report.

10. Domestic Violence: Orders of Protection and Restraining Orders. (2019, April 02). Retrieved August 13, 2020, from https://family.findlaw.com/domestic-violence/domestic-violence-orders-of-protection-and-restraining-orders.html.

11. Meyer, Jacob; Ellingson, Laura; Koltyn, Felli; Stegner, Aaron; Kim, Jee-seon; Cook, Dane, "Psychobiological Responses to Preferred and Prescribed Intensity Exercise in Major Depressive Disorder," *Medicine & Science in Sports & Exercise*: November 2016, Volume 48, Issue 11, p 2207–2215 doi: https://journals.lww.com/acsm-msse/Fulltext/2016/11000/Psychobiological_Responses_to_Preferred_and.17.aspx.

12. Puetz, Timothy & Flowers, Sara & O'Connor, Pat. (2008). "A Randomized Controlled Trial of the Effect of Aerobic Exercise Training on Feelings of Energy and Fatigue in Sedentary Young Adults with Persistent Fatigue." *Psychotherapy and Psychosomatics*, 77. 167–74. https://pubmed.ncbi.nlm.nih.gov/18277063/

13. Hjorth, Olof R., Andreas Frick, Malin Gingnell, Johanna M. Hoppe, Vanda Faria, Sara Hultberg, Iman Alaie, et al. "Expression and Co-Expression of Serotonin and Dopamine Transporters in Social Anxiety Disorder: a Multitracer Positron Emission Tomography Study." Nature News. Nature Publishing Group, December 10, 2019. https://www.nature.com/articles/s41380-019-0618-7#citeas.

14. Robinson, Lawrence, Melinda Smith, M.A., and Jeanne Segal, Ph.D. 2020. "Laughter Is the Best Medicine."*Help Guide.* October.

https://www.helpguide.org/articles/mental-health/laughter-is-the-best-medicine.htm.

15. "Influence of Exercise Intensity for Improving Depressed Mood in Depression: A Dose-Response Study." Meyer JD, Koltyn KF, Stegner AJ, Kim JS, Cook DB. *Behavior Therapy*. 2016 Jul;47(4):527-37. doi: 10.1016/j.beth.2016.04.003. Epub 2016, Apr 27, https://pubmed.ncbi.nlm.nih.gov/27423168/.

16. Bayes-Fleming, Nicole, et al. "Getting Started with Mindfulness."*Mindful*, Mindful Communications, 14 Sept. 2018, www.mindful.org/meditation/mindfulness-getting-started/.

17. "Guided Mindfulness Meditation, Series 1, Sitting Meditation." Performance by Jon Kabat-Zinn, BetterListen & WisdomFeed, 2017.*YouTube*, www.youtube.com/watch?v=I9Z4t9ZiUzM.

18. "Guided Body Scan Meditation for Mind & Body Healing." Performance by Michael Sealey, 2014. YouTube, www.youtube.com/watch?v=i7xGF8F28zo.

Acknowledgements

Every person has a vital foundation that shapes their character and reveals their identity. At age fourteen I took the naturalization Oath of Allegiance to the United States of America. Since that momentous ceremony, I have been motivated by the American dream. No matter what obstacles come my way, I believe I always have the opportunity to achieve my goals. Through these obstacles I learned attitude is a choice. I learned I am able to move past the abuse and pain and blossom into my own person.

This book was the work of many years of conversations, crying, reading, and thinking of profound issues. All of those moments had a huge impact on my way of life. I'd like to thank all my friends and foes for helping me develop into my authentic self.

Thank you to my best friend, Lisa Alimenti, my partner in crime. You have always encouraged me and supported all my eccentric ambitions. I am forever thankful for all your help in my life and in the creation of this book.

Thank you to my attorney, Nancy Southworth. I can't think of anyone else who I'd want to be by my side in a battle. You made a challenging case seem straightforward. It's rare to find a woman so elegantly fierce inside and outside the courtroom. I am honored to have been represented by you.

Thank you to Mathew Myers, my friend, my handyman, and the person I could always depend on for help. You are such a selfless man. Every day, you motivate me to be a better person.

Thank you to Joshua Kamp. You've always been there for me when things get tough. You've always provided me with excellent advice at the right moment.

Thank you to Jessica Bates. You gracefully brought my children and me into Christianity. We now walk in peace, free from our past and free from regrets. For this I am eternally grateful.

Finally, thank you to God, Creator of heaven and earth, the Author of meaning and purpose.

Photo Credit: Christopher R. Vasquez

Lydia Dominguez is currently serving as Technical Sergeant (TSgt) in the United States Air Force. She also holds a Bachelor of Arts in business management and has ten years of experience in human resources. Despite her professional background in human resources, she has a very emotional and comprehensive view on spousal violence, divorce, and rehabilitation. She relies on more than a decade of personal experience, as well as the stories of others who have been in similar situations, to educate and encourage abused women to escape their abusers and begin to recover. Her previous military experience and faith has infused the book with practical guidance and spiritual approaches that women may utilize when they are most in need.

During a twelve-year relationship, she attempted to escape her abuser seven times. Each time, Lydia was determined never to go back—until she did. She was affected by severe physical, emotional, and financial abuse. With her book *Don't Turn Back*, she hopes to promote empowerment, healing, and forgiveness.

Lydia now resides in Las Vegas, Nevada, with her two children. She considers her faith and family to be most important to her.

CPSIA information can be obtained
at www.ICGtesting.com
Printed in the USA
LVHW082343140821
695338LV00011B/882

9 780578 908991